The Movies
Go to College

The Movies
Go to College

Hollywood and the World of the College-Life Film

Wiley Lee Umphlett

Rutherford ● Madison ● Teaneck
Fairleigh Dickinson University Press
London and Toronto: Associated University Presses

Associated University Presses, Inc.
440 Forsgate Drive
Cranbury, NJ 08512

Associated University Presses
25 Sicilian Avenue
London WC1A 2QH, England

Associated University Presses
2133 Royal Windsor Drive
Unit 1
Mississauga, Ontario
Canada L5J 1K5

Library of Congress Cataloging in Publication Data

Umphlett, Wiley Lee, 1931–
  The movies go to college.

  Bibliography: p.
  Filmography: p.
  Includes index.
  1. College life films—United States—History and
criticism.   I. Title.
PN1995.9.C543U46   1984   791.43'09'09355   81-72048
ISBN 0-8386-3133-9

Printed in the United States of America

To my fellow "collegians"—past and present—whose featured roles in the ongoing drama of "college life" provided me with the real-life inspiration for this book.

Contents

Preface

What is there about the college-life movie that would make it deserving of a book-length appreciation? To be sure, a significantly large number of films of this type has appeared over the years, but, for one reason or another, we have never really taken this genre as seriously as we have, say, the Western, or the gangster film of the 1930s, or even the increasingly relevant science fiction movie. Even though higher education has played a prominent and important role in tempering American social experience, we have somehow tended to look upon it as not having had any meaningful relationship to or bearing on real life. Our conventional understanding holds that the educational process is characteristically cloistered and divorced from the realities of life. Thus since the 1920s the popular view has been that the social side of college life is the most representative and agreeable feature of the American collegiate experience.

But if the Hollywood movie can be considered a valid reflector of our popular tastes and values—and from our present perspective it increasingly appears to be—it would seem that there must be a great deal of social substance in a film genre that has enjoyed such a voluminous output since about 1915, and it should therefore be worthy of more attention. Intrigued by this supposition and motivated by my years in education as a student, teacher, and administrator, I set out to examine how movies inspired by the collegiate scene have revealed our changing social tastes and values over the years and to determine why these changes have taken place.

Of course, one of the first problems I encountered in writing *The Movies Go to College* was how to organize my discussion of the large number of college-life movies that have been produced over a roughly

9

sixty-five-year span. This quest prompted me at the outset to attempt a definition of the college-life film that would help determine the book's organizational pattern. For this book's purpose, then, I have defined the Hollywood film that is based entirely or partly on the collegiate experience as one in which the lead character or characters are socially motivated or conditioned by their immediate relationship with the environment of an American institution of higher learning to act or respond in a way that helps develop and/or resolve the film's dramatic conflict.

Naturally, this definition excludes the myriad films which deal with secondary and prep school life, as well as those films based primarily on foreign educational experience (for example, *A Yank at Oxford*), although such films may be referred to incidentally. I have omitted feature films that have been specially produced for television as well as movies that take place after the lead character or characters have departed the collegiate scene *(The Group, The Graduate)*, even though it is quite evident that this part of the characters' lives greatly influenced their personal development. On the other hand, my definition directed me to include borderline films like *The Gambler, Carnal Knowledge,* and *The Way We Were* simply because the collegiate experience of their central figures, as limited as it may be with respect to the total film's development, is very much in evidence and has a direct bearing on the characters' overall actions and dramatic significance.

The reader should note, too, that throughout this book the term *college* or *collegiate* is used collectively and interchangeably to refer primarily to the common educational and social experience of the student as well as to the complementary roles of the faculty, administration, and coaching staff of the institutions. These references may focus on the point of view of the student, the faculty member, the administrator, the athletic coach, or frequently they may include several or all postures within the same movie. Their special viewpoints tend to express themselves through five major forms and variations of the college-life genre: pure comedy, romantic comedy, musical comedy, pure drama, and melodrama. Of course, the plots of many collegiate films cut across these divisions to include common elements, particularly the one dealing with the spectacle of athletic activity, which has been such a predominant force in coloring the social side of the collegiate experience. For my overall purpose, though, the above categories are useful in observing and analyzing social behavior and the development of popular trends in the Hollywood version of college life over the years.

Admittedly, 1 have not covered all the college-life movies ever made—some of the earlier ones, unfortunately, are lost to posterity, and for convenience I have purposely ignored a number of the lesser vehicles—but I believe that those which are discussed here are representative enough to give the reader a solid feel for the significant periods in the development of the collegiate film: the 1920s, the 1930s, the 1940s–1950s, and the 1960s–1970s. The major sections of this book are devoted to each of these periods, and in each one I hope to demonstrate how this kind of film has been highly influential in embellishing our popular attitudes toward the college-life experience and our expectations of what this experience should be like—both in a fantasy and a real-life sense.

Over the course of the following sections, we will observe that the collegiate film has been as accurate an indicator and reflector of our cultural values and our popular fads and notions as any other recognized movie genre. This sensitivity is probably the result of the underlying inspiration for the college-life film in America. In contrast to the central focus of many other societal activities dramatized on film, the experience of attending college or relating in some way to its scene has attracted the special attention of Hollywood because the ultimate goal of the individual in undergoing this idealistic experience is to transform or revitalize the self—a characteristically American preoccupation generated by the intimate relationship of the individual to his or her societal setting. Throughout this book, then, the reader will observe this intimacy between the individual and the collegiate social environment contributing to some of Hollywood's finest as well as worst moments. Regardless of the level of quality ascribed to these films, one thing is certain to stand out in both the textual and pictorial content of this book: many of Hollywood's greatest and most popular stars, from the early days of John Wayne and Joan Crawford to the more recent times of George Segal and Glenda Jackson, have performed in a college-oriented movie.

Like the making of a movie, this book has been, in large part, a collaborative effort, and I am indebted to a number of people and agencies for their contributions to my research, particularly the following: Eddie Brandt and his fabulous movie still collection housed in the Saturday Matinee shop in North Hollywood, California; esteemed movie buff Harry Wilkinson of Marblehead, Massachusetts; the Academy of Motion Picture Arts and Sciences, Beverly Hills, California; The American Film Institute, Washington, D.C.; the John C. Pace Library of the University of West Florida in Pensacola; and, to be sure, the movie studios themselves who, ever responsive to realizing our social preoccupations as well as satisfying our fantasy appetites, produced the films that are the subject of this book.

The University of West Florida
Pensacola

The Movies
Go to College

1 Origins: The Collegiate Experience and the World of the College-Life Movie

Gaudeamus igitur,
Juvenes dum sumus;
Gaudeamus igitur,
Juvenes dum sumus;
Post jucundam juventutem,
Post malestam senectutem.
Nos habebit humus,
Nos habebit humus.
—traditional college song

After the severe intellectual labors of the day it is a not infrequent custom of the ingenuous youth of Harvard to refresh the weary mind with convivial ale, the social oyster, jolly songs, and conversation upon topics of less profundity than those that usually occupy the thoughts of young truth-seekers. . . .

—William Tucker Washburn,
Fair Harvard: A Story of American College Life (1869)

When you're in college, college life seems big and all the rest of the world so small that what you want to do as a student seems to be the only important thing in life. . . .

—George Fitch,
At Good Old Siwash (1911)

During the 1920s—that legendary period in American social history which so dramatically portrayed this country's ongoing love affair with material possessions and social success—the popular portrait of the college student was colored by certain characteristic preoccupations. Such accoutrements as raccoon coats, flapper dress styles, liquor flasks, and fast cars were always limned, it seemed, against a social background of wild fraternity parties and bacchanalian football weekends. Because of this romantic fascination with a supposedly high-living, glamorized life-style, public interest in the college-age set was unusually high at this time. In 1925, as if in response to the craze, Harold Lloyd, one of the silent film's all-time comedy greats, starred in a college-life feature film called *The Freshman* (Pathé). Ironically, many contemporary critics dissected this release as one of Lloyd's inferior movies, but the public, as usual, trusted its own critical instincts and flocked to *The Freshman* in droves.

From the moment Lloyd steps off the train at Tate College, audiences were enthralled by his portrayal of Harold "Speedy" Lamb, a social misfit who encounters a series of problems resulting from his misconception of the way things are in contrast to the way he thinks things should be. For example, he assumes that the crowd of students at the station is his welcoming committee when in reality the group has come to cheer the football hero's arrival. Following this incident, Speedy endures a succession of devastating social blunders, the significance of which ultimately transcends a comic view of college life in the 1920s to satirize the American obsession with projecting a successful social image. This perception of Americans' basic fear of being unpopular reveals both a clue to understanding a dominant side of our nature and the key to interpreting Hollywood's cinematic version of our collegiate traditions.

Among the plethora of college-life films produced during Hollywood's silent film era, a number of them, including *The Freshman,* reflect the obsession for social activity and help explain why the collegiate experience held such a fascination at that time. These movies also point to the film variations, extensions, and reactions that would naturally follow. There had been some prototypal efforts prior to the 1920s—which will be discussed shortly—but by the middle of the decade two general types of collegiate films were predominant: the romantic comedy and the sports melodrama. Typically, though, athletic activity was so integral to the plot of the college-life movie of this era that it often comes through in the romantic comedies, even those in which women are the central figures. For example, in *The Campus Flirt* (Famous Players, 1926), Bebe Daniels, a female counterpart to Speedy Lamb of *The Freshman,* is compelled to become a winner at sports in order to be popular with her classmates. As a society girl who has been spoiled by her mother, Bebe is sent to college by her well-meaning father so that she can obtain a more democratic exposure to life. Because of her stuck-up airs, though, Bebe has a difficult time coming across as a real person to her fellow students, and it is not until she makes the women's track team

Harold Lloyd's archetypal role in *The Freshman* (Pathé, 1925) focused on a first-year student's efforts to be popular with his classmates. This campus drugstore scene is typical of his bumbling attempts to ingratiate himself with his fellow students.

and learns the meaning of sportsmanship that she finally achieves popularity. Significantly, the personal conflicts of the individual are resolved by the social demands of the system.

The film version of George Ade's popular play, *The Fair Co-ed* (MGM, 1927), was based on a similar social predicament in which a self-centered student (Marion Davies) attends college mainly to capture the affections of the handsome young basketball coach (Johnny Mack Brown), only to find that the other co-eds have the same idea. After joining the team, though, Miss Davies learns the difference between her own selfish interests and the value of team play. The end result is that she discovers what it means to win the big game as well as the attentions of her coach.

Other key collegiate films of the time also functioned as socially oriented models to be emulated. In Ade's archetypal *The College Widow* (Warner Bros., 1927), which had appeared on film as early as 1915, Delores Costello inspired the plot situation for a host of later movies in her role of a college girl committed to recruiting a winning football team. The reason? Her father, an individual dedicated to old-fashioned academic excellence, will lose his job as president of the college if he doesn't come up with a team that can beat the school's big rival. Why the president instead of the coach should be responsible for this mandate is never made clear, but the board of trustees clearly states its case: the college has been losing students by putting too much emphasis on education instead of athletics. Taking this cue, the enterprising Miss Costello proceeds to sign up the best players she can find, enticing each one into thinking that she is the number-one love of his life. When the players discover that she has been stringing them along, they threaten to boycott the big game, but after the "college widow" confesses that her true intention was to save her father's job, the team members decide to rally behind her. In fact, they go on to win the game, and things apparently turn out happily for everybody except Miss Costello, who has collected so many boy friends by this time that she ironically winds up without that special one.[1] Such was the inanity of the period's sports-oriented film plots; however, some of them, like *The College Widow,* came across as low-keyed, occasionally unintentional satires of an educational system that apparently had lost sight of its mission.

More rare were school-life films on the order of *Naughty but Nice* (First National, 1927), in which Colleen Moore must prove her individual worth and social acceptance without ever resorting to athletics. As a naïve country-girl attending a fancy finishing school, Miss Moore is propelled headlong into a series of Lloyd-like social clashes before she comes up with a clearer perspective of herself in relation to her social world.[2]

Basically, the inspiration for the college-life movie can be attributed to Hollywood's reaction to the natural conflict between the assumptions of American idealism and the demands of social reality. Capitalizing on the conventional understanding that the collegiate environment is expressly designed for American youth to pursue its ideals and personal dreams, the representative college-life movie reveals that a student's ideals and dreams often do not measure up to the realities created by our system of higher education. Typically, too, movie professors and administrators have to deal with this inconsistency between ideals and reality. Expressed primarily through comedy—particularly comedy tempered by a mood of satire or burlesque—the college-life movie, with its peculiar sensitivity to social involvement and expression, has been highly popular and prolific over the years. Since Harold Lloyd's comic capers in the 1920s, moviegoers of each decade have been regaled by this type of film, including the irreverent barbs of the Marx Brothers in *Horse Feathers* (Paramount, 1932); the screwball comedy atmosphere of *The Male Animal* (Warner Bros., 1942); the musical comedy antics of Betty Grable (one of the genre's most durable stars) in *How to Be Very, Very Popular* (20th Century-Fox, 1955); Jerry Lewis's Jekyll-

The "college widow," a stock role in the college-life movie, was often lonely, as this pose of Delores Costello in *The College Widow* (Warner Bros., 1927) suggests. In her zeal to win over superior athletes to her school, the college-widow type usually failed to win a fellow for herself.

Hyde portrayal of the stereotypical college instructor in *The Nutty Professor* (Paramount, 1963); and in the 1970s, the sardonic hedonism of the fraternity brothers of *Animal House* (Universal City, 1978). In recent years, audiences have also been entertained by a significant number of apparently serious films with college-oriented backgrounds: *Who's Afraid of Virginia Woolf?* (Warner Bros., 1966), *Getting Straight* (Columbia, 1970), *The Paper Chase* (20th Century-Fox,

1973), and *Lost and Found* (Columbia, 1979), to name several of the more outstanding ones. Even these films, as latently serious as they appear to be, frequently take on a comic perspective due to their exaggerated sense of social behavior. Essentially, they are all based on the college-life movie's characteristic emphasis on the conflict between the individual and his or her social setting.

The primary inspirational source for all this—the institution of the American college or university—was already over 250 years old when the motion picture began to develop as an entertainment form early in this century. As with other kinds of film drama, the legitimate stage supplied a variety of story sources for the early college-life film—for example, the plays of George Ade *(The College Widow, The Fair Co-ed)* and William DeMille *(Classmates)*—but the more expansive form of fiction doubtless provided the greater inspiration. As early as 1869 we can detect the seeds for a college-life film tradition in William Tucker Washburn's *Fair Harvard: A Story of American College Life,* with its social emphasis on students' boisterous extracurricular involvement in sports, dormitory pranks, and heroic drinking bouts. Around the turn of the century, Charles Macomb Flandrau and Owen Wister, also inspired by a Harvard atmosphere, produced, respectively, *The Diary of a Freshman* (1901) and *Philosophy Four* (1903). These popular stories with a social slant were closer in time to the first college-life movies, and therefore probably had more influence on the genesis of the films than did earlier works. Even turn-of-the-century sports fiction—particularly that of Ralph Henry Barbour, which dramatized inspirational school and college experience for a juvenile audience—must have had some influence on Hollywood's idealized approach to the role of athletics in college life. However, Owen Johnson's 1912 novel, *Stover at Yale,* undoubtedly afforded the movie people one of their most reliable sources for interpreting college athletics because of its realistic treatment of that favorite American literary theme of the individual versus the system. In trying out for the Yale football team, the hero of this novel is appalled at the seriousness of the competition for places on the team. Consequently, he perceives that the intercollegiate athletic system is specially designed to control the will of the individual, meaning that a successful player is often compelled to sacrifice his personal ideals to the demands of the system. This compromise is one that many a central figure of a college-life movie will make, but not all these characters are students; many are faculty members, administrators, or even coaches.

Throughout the abundant variations of this basic plot situation in the college-life film, an underlying feeling of mistrust is commonly revealed by an individual character whenever he or she must confront the system, whether its demands are expressed through antagonists like an instructor, a coach, the administration, or even the institution itself. Because of its sensitivity to this dramatic conflict, the college-life film has always had more to say about what we may expect of the collegiate experience than what the real-life institutions themselves have ever had to say about it. In this book, then, I propose to examine the import of this distinction and to analyze chronologically what the movies' interpretation of collegiate experience, whether fantasized or realistic, tells us about our changing social values and their effect on our expectations and perceptions of one of the most pervasive but misunderstood American social experiences.

Historically, venerable institutions of learning like Harvard and Yale have exemplified in their own expanding missions what has happened to the course of higher education in this country, particularly as it has responded to the changing needs of successive generations of students. Although the establishment of American higher education had as its original objective the training of young males for the clergy and the professions, it obviously and naturally lost sight of this primary goal as our society became more diverse and complex. Nonetheless, these institutions have managed to retain the honorable intent of their original missions while branching out in an infinite number of directions to offer to all minority groups, including women, preparation for the professions and for a variety of technological-commercial careers and vocations.

In addition to having become a credentializing agency for the professions and the vocations, the college/university establishment has evolved into a highly visible means to an end, symbolized, of course, by the college degree with its built-in opportunity for economic and social mobility. Oddly enough, in the movies the rationale for earning a college degree is seldom expressed outright, but it is often implied. Even the well-to-do student can come across to the viewer as an individual who belongs to an exceptionally dedicated and select group—one that is deserving of our special attention.[3] In spite of the chaotic and disruptive developments of recent years, the college student's purposeful experience still symbolizes the American quest for dream fulfillment, and as a result the campus persists as a place of dream pursuit. It is also where, traditionally, the student has come not so much for the intangibles of intellectual stimulation or vocational guidance as for the more real concerns of social identity and companionship and, as expressed in the prototypal fiction of William Tucker Washburn, for just plain innocent fun or perhaps even a little hell raising.

Responding to an increasingly liberal mood, American fiction writers of the 1920s did not hesitate to draw on the vagaries of college life in particular to comment on what they thought was wrong with modern life in general. In fact, a large number of college-life novels

You don't know the half of "It" until you see and *hear* Clara speak from the screen in her latest wild adventure at college with her gang of dazzling darlings of the "dorms." Double the appeal of any other Bow picture.

Clara **BOW** *invites you to* "THE WILD PARTY"

her first ALL-TALKING picture. By the author of "Flaming Youth." Directed by Dorothy Arzner.

A Paramount ALL-TALKING *Picture*

This ad for a 1929 Clara Bow movie focuses on the new-found liberation of the co-ed and provides us with a social metaphor for the collegiate experience during the 1920s.

appeared during this era, with some of the most significant works coming out during the first half of the decade. Written by authors not long out of college themselves, most of these novels were mediocre, but two well-received works of the period actually contributed a great deal to the popular conception of the supposedly flaming-youth lifestyle of the college student. They also had a powerful effect on the way that the movie people would interpret the college-life experience. Both F. Scott Fitzgerald's *This Side of Paradise* (1920) and Percy Marks's *The Plastic Age* (1924), while distinctively different in concept and literary style, expressed a common criticism of the educational process as doing very little to prepare one for the realities of life. Whether expressed from the point of view of the aesthete (Fitzgerald's Amory Blaine) or the average student (Marks's Hugh Carver), both these novels insinuated that the most meaningful experiences at college occurred not in the classroom but in bull sessions, social events, and athletic competitions. As a result, most traditional academicians were lampooned or satirized in these novels while those who espouse bold and controversial ideas were adulated and romanticized for maintaining their individuality within the system.[4]

Typically, the predominant attitude of college-life fiction since the 1920s, and one which has carried over to the movies, suggests that we can learn more about life through our direct relationships with people than we can through any artificial contact we might have through books and the classroom. It is an obvious anti-intellectual posture which informs readers and viewers that the traditional college is remote from the real world in a societal sense—is, in fact, an unreal community run by impractical dullards. Although this complaint had been voiced ever since the collegiate institution's earliest days, no amount of criticism has ever managed to abolish the idealized popular view of the college campus as a place where personal dreams can be meaningfully realized.

Paradoxically, though, the collegiate institution itself has had to be concerned with much more than just pursuing its idealistic and socializing roles. It has also had to live with incisive criticism and disruptive social change, and to take on challenging new responsibilities as institutional missions have become redefined—all this in order to meet the educational demands of an ever-changing society while naturally resisting the ultimate democratization of its educational traditions. In general, the college-life film tradition reflects the reaction of the college campus to these changes over the years, especially as mirrored by student behavior. In another sense, the college-life film reveals the collegiate institution's dedication to the constant ideal that has helped it transcend the problems of political discord and internal conflict continually cropping up among its major units of organization—the governing board, the administration, the faculty, the support staff, and, naturally, the student body.

Of these groups, the students have traditionally been the most vociferous, contentious, and rebellious within the system, and as a result have at times contributed their fair share to disrupting and complicating the educational process, whether their causes have been justified or not. The once seemingly unassailable authority of the administration was so eroded by student demands in the 1970s that today many feel it is the students, not the administration, who run the institution. Indeed, students have come to possess more of a share in institutional governance, a development that the films conditioned by the mood of the late 1960s—*R.P.M.* (Columbia, 1970), *Drive, He Said* (Columbia, 1971), *Getting Straight* (Columbia, 1970), and *The Strawberry Statement* (MGM, 1970)—presaged through their highly dramatic approach to students' militant stands during that tumultuous period. But the intrainstitutional clashes that these movies visualized in such a graphically sensational manner were really not too foreign or uncommon to the campus scene, for in actuality they had grown out of a longtime natural enmity generated by the customary *in loco parentis* relationship between student and administration. Traditionally, students have been an unruly, disobedient, and thoroughly disrespectful lot in the face of authority. In spite of the code of the college gentleman that many schools have fostered, particularly in the East and the South, many a rambunctious scholar who eventually gained respectable standing and high position in later life must have caused his dean a few anxious moments as well as an occasional sleepless night by neglecting the educational process in favor of sowing a few wild oats. The metaphorical relationship that has always existed between administration and student is akin to that of a parent exercising his natural right to discipline, while the child, in turn, looks for any opportunity to cross up the parent. Right from the start, this predicament provided the movie people with an inherently dramatic situation for their special interpretation of college life.

Another factor contributing to the students' natural sense of rebellion and alienation is that the college years in America represent a kind of limbo in one's life. The standard college-age years of eighteen to twenty-two represent a bleak hiatus between awkward adolescence and mature adulthood—a characteristically confusing time when one gropes toward self-discovery, most commonly and often disappointingly through sexual adventure and social experimentation. However, in most earlier college-life movies, particularly those of the 1930s, viewers may find themselves hard-pressed to detect a negative attitude toward experience; in fact, these films seem obsessed with a fantasized, almost mythical revelation of youth as the best time in life. To reinforce this attitude, films like *The Sweetheart of Sigma Chi* (Monogram, 1933), *Old Man Rhythm* (RKO, 1935), *College Holiday* (Paramount, 1936), and *Varsity Show* (Warner Bros., 1937) concentrate on glamorous settings that include an endless parade of beautiful co-eds, a bountiful supply of handsome athletes who always seem to be on the winning side, and the entertaining escapades of the popularly conceived college man. Such films make these characters even more attractive and exotic by dwelling on their social preoccupation with behavior fads, novel clothing styles, sporting events, and on occasion a form of orgiastic revelry—the kind of experience, it seems, that would apprise audiences of not only the appealing but also the exciting side of the American college student's social image.

The enactment of the Land Grant College Act of 1862 and the attendant growth and expansion of the American university system in the latter half of the nineteenth century began a trend toward the ultimate democratization of the collegiate experience. Although many radical changes would characterize higher education over the next one-hundred years, the masses of people would continue to look

Paramount Studios, the most prolific producer of college-life movies during the 1930s, glamorized the social side of the collegiate scene by displaying the beautiful co-ed—here, in a publicity still for *Pigskin Parade* (1936).

upon the college experience as an elitist endeavor whose only practical value lay in the opportunity to secure a share of the American economic pie. In the process of preparing for their fair cut, though, students began to slight their studies by placing an increased emphasis on social activity as an essential part of the college experience. Naturally, popular models for this kind of social behavior sprang up, in particular that eastern undergraduate tradition which dictated the standards for the "college man"—the upperclassman who affected a delicate balance between youthful spontaneity and worldly sophistication. His was a posture carefully cultivated and displayed in dress, talk, mannerisms, and a sensitivity to social activity or a degree of athletic ability or both.

Established around the turn of the century in the popular fiction of Charles Macomb Flandrau, Owen Wister, and George Fitch the model had evolved by the 1920s into the character of Amory Blaine in F. Scott Fitzgerald's novel, *This Side of Paradise* (1920), a major part of which takes place at Princeton. Amory's pose, much more sophisticated than that which would later evolve in fiction and the movies, suggested that what was learned in the classroom, if anything, was to be purposely suppressed unless it had social or personal application to life, literature, and the arts. One should never confess to learning anything from a system; in fact, Amory intimates, intelligent judgment should spring spontaneously and intuitively from one's inner being. At heart, then, this prototypal version of the modern college man, even though it fostered its own degree of conformity within the code itself, was an anti-intellectual expression of the individual versus the system. As the outward sign of this confrontation, the dress code varied from the trendsetting formal styles of the Ivy League to the more relaxed dress of the South, Midwest, and far West, but the studied attitudes and affected mannerisms of the college man were universal and represented a social role that the college-life movie has singled out for special delineation over the years. Whether a sophisticate, an athlete, big-man-on-campus, or merely a party boy, the role has attracted through the years the varying talents of performers like William Haines, Richard Arlen, Lew Ayres, Robert Young, Mickey Rooney, Ryan O'Neal, and John Belushi.[5]

The macho appeal of college football was a theme of *Maker of Men* (Columbia, 1931). John Wayne and Ward Bond listen to the exhortations of coach Jack Holt.

Team sports, particularly football, have also made a major contribution to the popular conception of the collegiate experience and the social image of the college man. Football, which fantasized and mythologized the heroic symbol of the varsity athlete, was a powerful attraction for male students even before the introduction of subsidized sports programs. From the highly romanticized portrait of Princeton's all-round Hobey Baker in the teens to the mass-publicized image of a specialized running back like Georgia's Herschel Walker in the 1980s, college football has captured the American imagination through its projection of the player as a rugged individualist whose mobility is tempered by our fascination with goal-oriented strategy and opportunistic action. With the introduction of football as an intercollegiate sport during the latter half of the last century, the obsessive dream of many a young male was to "make" the varsity team and, of course, bring honor to his school as well as himself by performing gloriously and heroically on the gridiron. Although many of the young men who went out for the team in the earlier days of intercollegiate sports were socially motivated by a mind set akin to that of Harold Lloyd in *The Freshman,* they also displayed a patriotic sense of duty and service that inspired them to give their all for their schools. Paradoxically, those candidates fortunate enough to be chosen as varsity athletes enjoyed a campus-wide prestige and identity that the classroom scholar could never hope to attain. Accordingly, the movies quickly recognized the fact that accomplishment through athletic action and physical effort has greater appeal to the American imagination than does achievement in scholarship and the arts. Thus, most early films of college life depict athletic heroes who rarely refer to their studies—and, in fact, never seem to have time to go to class. Not until the realistic movement of the post–World War II film and the development of a dramatically rounded character like Steve Novak (John Derek) in *Saturday's Hero* (Columbia, 1951) were audiences introduced to a football player who appears to be equally interested in his studies as in his performance on the field.

Not only was the college-age male inspired to seek out sports to express his manhood, school loyalty, and social identity, but by the close of the nineteenth century, college alumni and the general public had generated a large following for intercollegiate sports, particularly football. In fact, football soon grew so popular as a spectator sport that by 1903 Harvard boasted a stadium seating fifty-seven thousand people. Not to be outdone, Yale by 1914 had built a bowl that could hold seventy-five thousand. Developing simultaneously with this widespread interest in college athletics was a patriotic devotion to one's school and a fervent pride in the area it represented—attitudes that continue to the present day. This is particularly true in the South,

A rare scene—football players actually attending class—in *The Spirit of Notre Dame* (Universal, 1931). Andy Devine responds as Lew Ayres and William Bakewell (directly in front) contemplate.

a region which since the Civil War has undoubtedly felt more cause to express and identify itself through superior athletic teams. Football, which has stood out as the most exemplary game to reveal this intimate relationship between school and region, has played a large part in indoctrinating the general public to the concept of sport as entertainment. It was only natural for the movies to follow this lead, and sports became one of the strongest inspirational sources for the college-life movie, as evidenced in its projection of the "Big Game"—a communal event of almost religious intensity that spiritually unites athletes, student body, faculty, alumni, and often an entire region or state.[6] In the prodigious number of college-life films that have appeared since the 1920s, the big game was usually the climactic point of the plot, highlighted by the featured school's star player (and sometimes lowly scrub) coming on to score the winning touchdown and keep the honor of the school untarnished. This ritualistic scene permeated the silent film era, and peaked in the 1930s with, for example, a movie actually called *The Big Game* (RKO, 1936). It resurfaced as recently as 1979 in *Fast Break* (Columbia), although here the spirit of the big game is projected through the sport of basketball.[7]

The sports flavor of many of the seminal college-life movies of the 1920s was enhanced by their dependence on a well-known athlete of the time appearing in a starring or supporting role as, for example, dashman Charlie Paddock as Bebe Daniels's coach in *The Campus Flirt;* Johnny Mack Brown, the Alabama all-American, in *The Fair Co-ed;* and Guinn "Big Boy" Williams, a rodeo performer and supposedly one-time member of the Oklahoma football team, as one of the players in *The College Widow*. Reflecting the mass-entertainment appeal and attraction of the big-name athlete, the college sports dramas of the 1920s instigated one of Hollywood's biggest star-making traditions by signing some of the era's greatest sports personalities.[8] This innovation paid off handsomely in a number of cases, for a star athlete invariably turned out to be more popular than the movie stars themselves, thereby assigning low-keyed films a magnetic box office attraction they would never otherwise have had. A good example of this sort of magic appeal was *One Minute to Play* (Film Booking Office, 1926), in which Red Grange, the sensational all-American halfback from the University of Illinois, ironically is cast in the role of a college man who refuses to play football because he has secretly promised his father that he won't. Peer pressure finally persuades him to join the team, but the wealthy father learns of his son's decision and threatens to cut off the school's endowment if Red continues to play. Knowing that the college needs financial support, Red quits just before the big game, but at this point the plot takes a sudden turn. Red's father shows up for his first football game and discovers that the game isn't so bad after all. He then approves of his son's playing, and Red comes on to score a touchdown and kick an extra point to win the game in the final seconds. In his first movie role, Grange turned in a surprisingly good performance, demonstrating that he could carry a romantic interest as well as a pigskin. Ironically enough, the scriptwriter for this film obviously had some difficulty in coming up with a credible athletic situation that could outdo Grange's amazing real-life heroics on the gridiron.[9]

The year 1926—the heart of the so-called Golden Age of Sport—was a banner one for silent sports films, and two of the best of the collegiate variety were *The Quarterback* (Famous Players) and *Brown of Harvard* (MGM), a remake of the Essanay 1917 version based on the original play. "All football stories are built on the same formula," wrote a contemporary film reviewer, "the hero making a grandstand finish for the winning touchdown despite any complication."[10] This observation certainly holds up overall, but the basic quality that distinguished these two films from their competition was their comparative realism, which was fairly well conceived for their day in spite of Richard Dix's impossible forward pass in the final twenty seconds for the winning edge in *The Quarterback,* and Wil-

Real-life football star Red Grange proved to his fans that he could act as well as play football in *One Minute to Play* (Film Booking Office, 1926). Mary McAllister is the girl.

liam Haines's last-quarter drive for victory against Yale in *Brown of Harvard*. Although these films relied heavily on the excitement of athletic competition for their dramatic intensity, they rose above the usual trappings of the sports oriented film through their honest attempts to portray meaningful social relationships both on and off the field. In *Brown of Harvard,* the romantic rivalry between Haines and Francis X. Bushman for a professor's daughter (Mary Brian) is extended to the field of competition, where screen realism is greatly enhanced by actual location shots—an accomplishment quite rare for a time that depended mainly on newsreel footage to project the spirit of athletic struggle.[11]

William Haines was cast in another collegiate feature film later in the decade, this one a sound movie called *The Duke Steps Out* (MGM, 1929). This picture's unique approach to sports, as far as college-life films are concerned, has Haines performing not as a football player but as a prize fighter who wants to prove his mettle to his wealthy father. As he works toward his most important match, he falls for co-ed Joan Crawford, who, in the traditional female role of the collegiate film serves both to enhance and complicate the social side of Haines's life.[12]

Beginning in the 1920s, it became obvious to many that the special treatment of college athletes smacked of professionalism. Nevertheless, they were idolized and revered by the public as symbols of the ideals that the college and community represented. Newspapers, magazines, and in time radio and television, in their attempts to keep a growing legion of sports fans across the nation informed, acknowledged the unique and powerful appeal of the college athlete through their formulation of all-America teams and top-team rankings. As a result, the news media have always been a strong influence in molding the public's conception of what college sports (and, by extension, the collegiate experience itself) are all about. But the movies, with their power to mythologize both the extraordinary and the commonplace, have probably more than any other force conditioned us to assume that college athletics have an obligatory role in enhancing the image of the school they represent. We can conclude that college athletics, particularly as the Hollywood film has interpreted them, have been highly instrumental in indoctrinating and conditioning both the general public and college-bound youth to a common understanding (whether fantasized or real) of what the college experience should be like.

Other factors of a more subtle and psychological nature affected the attitudes of students, educators, and the moviemakers not only toward the college experience but toward life itself. Along with the increasing interest in science and experimental methodology in the nineteenth century, new fields and related subject areas began to be added to college curricula. In marked contrast to what one might be expected to learn from traditional subjects of classical languages, philosophy, rhetoric, and theology, the new subjects stressed "experience" as the major determining criterion in both scientific reasoning and in human relationships. The result of this revolutionary new emphasis was a gradual turning away from the religious values that had been the cornerstones of the first institutions of higher learning in this country. Even the oldest institutions gradually shifted their objectives in response to a growing social consciousness, and like the newer colleges, came to define their roles in terms of current social realities. Accordingly, the twentieth century saw the social sciences of psychology and sociology added to the curriculum. At the same

A Touchdown! *featuring the*
ALL-AMERICAN FOOTBALL TEAM

What is behind the success of a great football team? Men? Teamwork? Coaching? Watch Joan Bennett vamp the whole All-American team into playing for her and you'll agree that sometimes —"Maybe it's Love!"

Coach Howard Jones
Univ. of So. Cal.
W. K. Schoonover
Arkansas
E. N. Sleight
Purdue
George Gibson
Minnesota
Tim Moynihan
Notre Dame
Ray Montgomery
Pittsburgh

Based on the story by
Mark Canfield
Screen play and dialogue by
Joseph Jackson

Otto Pommerening
Michigan
Kenneth Haycraft
Minnesota
Russell Saunders
Univ. of So. Cal.
Howard Harpster
Carnegie Tech.
Paul Scull
Univ. of Penn.
William Banker
Tulane

Directed by
WILLIAM WELLMAN
Director of "Wings"

featuring
JOE E. BROWN JOAN BENNETT JAMES HALL

WARNER BROS. present
Maybe It's Love
A WARNER BROS. AND VITAPHONE PICTURE

This magazine ad for a 1930 Joe E. Brown movie illustrates the prominent part real-life football celebrities played in the movies during this era.

time, college instructors developed an increasingly liberal attitude toward "life adjustment" problems and the rewards of immediate experience. This new attitude held that a fuller, freer social life was an important, if not essential, adjunct to the serious business of attending lectures, reading books, and writing papers. Viewing a college-life musical of the 1930s like *Collegiate* leads us to believe that going to college in that day apparently consisted of nothing more than social activity, since Jack Oakie, the college dean, insists that his students' efforts should be directed primarily toward learning how to sing and dance. Obviously, the free-wheeling conventions of the Hollywood musical, which allowed for all kinds of wacky goings on, were operating at full capacity in this film.

Just as the students had originated the various sporting endeavors to provide themselves with a much-needed physical and emotional outlet, they in turn established the clubs, the secret societies, and the fraternity-sorority system to allow for social expression and interaction. These groups were highly instrumental in loosening the behavior standards between the sexes—a situation very much in evidence by the end of World War I. This was a time, of course, that many historians look back upon as a point of demarcation in our social

In *Collegiate* (Paramount, 1936), social-life classes took priority over academic pursuits—apparently a fantasized reaction to the real-life concerns of the Depression era.

history, representing not only our international coming of age but also the passing of an older, more innocent and conventional way of life. Accordingly, the scene was set on our college campuses for the development of an infinitely more liberal attitude toward sexual behavior and social expectations.

Co-educational institutions flourished in the 1920s, and the college woman or "co-ed" began to assert herself as a social force, with the result that behavior between the sexes was expressed in more ways than just through social dancing and drinking. Husband hunting became a popular sport, and in *The Wild Party* (Paramount, 1929), Clara Bow's seductive manner is sufficient to make a professor (Fredric March) quit his position and take off after her. *College Coquette* (First National, 1929) presented its version of the liberated female in Ruth Taylor, who decides that instead of a professor she'll go after the football coach.

The increasing availability of automobiles aided romantic relationships considerably by giving students more than just a newfound mobility; it provided them with an immediate means to sexual expres-

Fredric March, in one of his first movie roles, plays a college professor in *The Wild Party* (Paramount, 1929) who is smitten by the uninhibited charms of Clara Bow (second from right).

sion, whether through group "petting" bouts or the more private affair of "going all the way." Appropriately, the automobile in the movies of the 1920s and 1930s is a vivid symbol of individual freedom and sexual abandon. The scene of laughing, carefree students gadding about in an open roadster is a significantly common one in these films, and although the behavior depicted is dated and absurdly innocent when compared to a more recent film like *The Strawberry Statement* (MGM, 1970) in which sex is openly expressed, it nonetheless represents a breaking away from conventional behavior. Eventually, this kind of activity evolved into the uninhibited sexual license and expression in the films of the 1960s and 1970s. The movies have always capitalized on society's futile attempts to suppress and control sexual behavior, and the college-life movie, from *The Plastic Age* (Commonwealth, 1925) to *First Love* (Paramount, 1977), has always been one of the more sensitive forms for expressing this condition.

Like *The Plastic Age, The Wild Party* also reflected Hollywood's reaction to the new code of sexual behavior. Both films were vehicles for Clara Bow (1905–65), one of the screen's most pervasive sex symbols during the flapper era and a popular image of the kind of girl the public must have thought was attending college at this time. The fact that Miss Bow was the choice to play a co-ed in both these films tells us much about Hollywood's quest to give movie audiences what it thought they wanted. Crowned by her eye-catching red hair, which unfortunately did not come across as vividly in the predominant black-and-white films of the time, Clara nonetheless struck quite a figure with her bobbed hair, short skirts, rolled stockings, and vibrantly full body. During the height of her popularity, the mid-1920s, she projected a magic personal quality known popularly as "It." Coined by British writer Elinor Glyn, the term conjured forth a fortunate combination of spirited vitality and common good looks, both of which Clara Bow was thought to have in bountiful supply.

In *The Plastic Age,* for example, Clara represents the so-called emancipated female of her day who is beginning to smoke, drink, and perhaps share herself sexually with whomever might be right for the moment—at least such is the kind of behavior suggested by the story line. This screen version of Percy Marks's best-selling novel may have taken some liberties in its transcription to film, but it was reasonably successful with both the critics and the moviegoers, while its critical tone looked ahead to the iconoclastic collegiate film of the 1960s and 1970s.[13] Both athletics and the obligatory profusion of good-looking co-eds come in for their stock treatment, but it is Clara Bow's triangular relationship with good-guy Donald Keith and bad-guy Gilbert Roland that holds the story together. Although Miss Bow's collegiate life-style appears rather tame by later standards, the public no doubt assumed that in the behavior of this popular star it

In the college-life movie of the 1920s and 1930s, the automobile was more than a status symbol; it was the ultimate means of social expression. Above, Jack Oakie and Mary Carlisle, with Richard Arlen at the wheel, and Mary Kornman in *College Humor* (Paramount, 1933).

was seeing the so-called sensational side of college life in the 1920s.

Like most short-lived promotional rages that attain mass appeal and interest, though, the image of Clara Bow was fading by 1929 when she made *The Wild Party,* a film whose title could easily have been a metaphor for her own private life rather than for the social side of college life. Due to her obsessive gambling and sexual indiscretions, which included affairs with a long line of well-known men, Miss Bow became a favorite target of her day's smut tabloids and magazines.[14] Partly for this reason, *The Wild Party* was looked upon by many as the most sensational interpretation of the collegiate side of the era of the Charleston, hip-flask booze, and group necking parties. More significantly, this film brought to the fore the acting ability of Fredric March, who plays the role of an anthropology professor more interested in the charms of Miss Bow than he is in his academic duties. His assessment of the four years one spends at college as "one wild party" undoubtedly represented the general view of the time, and as such must have gone a long way in conditioning moviegoers' opinions of life at college in the 1920s.[15]

Other noteworthy films of the 1920s, reflecting the era's more liberal license to interpret social behavior, tried to expand upon what had already been done in the college-life genre, but *The Drop Kick* (First National, 1927) turned out to be nothing more than a soap opera in which the football coach's wife tries to bed down with one of her husband's star players, Richard Barthelmess. Typically, *The College Hero* (Columbia, 1927) and *The Cheer Leader* (Lumas, 1928) came across as tired variations on the theme of "good old Podunk winning the big football game in the last two minutes of play," as one reviewer put it.[16] *The College Hero* did have one attractive feature, however; it featured Ben Turpin, one of the most popular clowns of the silent era.

Actually, the performances of two of Hollywood's greatest silent clowns will provide us with our most meaningful insights into the nature and intent of the American college-life movie: Harold Lloyd in *The Freshman* and Buster Keaton in *College* (United Artists, 1927). Produced by the Pathé studios, the Lloyd film not only capitalized on the general public's infatuation with college life during the 1920s, it dramatized the basic conflict between American idealism and social

The 1920s' social acceptance of co-eds indulging in alcoholic beverages appears to have aroused ill feelings between Gwen Lee (left) and Joan Crawford as their bemused boyfriends look on in *The Duke Steps Out* (MGM, 1929).

reality more perceptively than any other college-life film has before or since. Harold "Speedy" Lamb, the hero of *The Freshman,* is a small-town boy whose expectations of what the collegiate experience has to offer is so much a part of his social outlook that upon arriving at Tate College his every move is controlled by an obsessive drive for popularity and acceptance by his peers. The ironic predicament of Speedy's comically unique, yet socially representative manner derives from his self-centered dreams of what college should be like. Actually, his daydreams of success have been inspired by the fiction he's read, the movies he's seen, and the athletic heroes he's worshipped—particularly football stars like Tate's Chet Trask, who comes across to Speedy as the real-life embodiment of Frank Merriwell. The result is that Speedy interprets every social situation he confronts as having special meaning for his own privately defined world. Furthermore, he believes that his college associates see him as what he would like to be—very popular and exceptionally athletic—simply because the system has informed him that this is the way things are supposed to be. His social naïveté is evident when he shows up on campus wearing a varsity letter sweater, an act that would surely arouse the ire of any varsity performer who has already endured the rigors of winning his letter. Although his girl (Jobyna Ralston) keeps reminding him to "be yourself," it is obvious to viewers that the demands of the system have distorted his basic concept of his social self, and although he doesn't have one iota of athletic ability, his misconception of whatever abilities he does have tells him that the one sure way to achieve the status of big-man-on-campus is to become a football hero. Speedy has evidently come to the right school to test his mettle, too, for in one title satirizing the system Tate is described as "a large football stadium with a college attached."

At heart, the ironic social predicament of Speedy Lamb, which has been engendered by an unknowing and naïvely innocent relationship with those around him, tells us more about the nature of the American social experience than many a lengthy discourse can. On one level, his ambitious and doggedly dedicated attitudes reflect those of a legion of young males who have dreamed of playing for their school and becoming an instant hero by scoring the winning touchdown in the big game. One of the opening titles catches the mania perfectly: "Do you remember those boyhood days when going to College was greater than going to Congress—and you'd rather be Right Tackle than President?" On another level, the outrageous social antics of Speedy underscore a pervasive paradox of the American dream: dedication to an ideal does not guarantee social success, nor can popularity and social standing be always achieved through a winning performance, as most of us are wont to assume. Like so many of us in our obsession for chasing the dream, Speedy makes the mistake of ignoring the social realities with which he is involved.

On still another level, though, we are witness to a dramatic situation that lays bare the deception of a system that suggests that the ability to make the team is the epitome of success. To become a varsity performer in any intercollegiate sport demands that one meet a high standard of talent, to be sure, but the very ineptness of Speedy Lamb as a football player not only contributes to some of *The Freshman's* funniest moments, it also criticizes the team play or organizational concept that Speedy has been influenced by and wants so much to be a part of. To emphasize his overeager posture, sight gags—a Lloyd trademark—abound. One of the best and most perceptive of these in the entire film finds Speedy, after a jarring tackle, sprawled next to a tackling dummy, wondering if the disjointed leg he sees next to himself is his own or the dummy's. As a visual reminder of his disorientation within the system, such comic incongruities help audiences to identify with Speedy's plight. The basis for the film's humor and its satirical edge develops naturally from this rapport.

Even though his dogged persistence does earn himself the job of team manager, Speedy continues to think of himself as a playing member of the team, and on the day of the big game he finally gets his

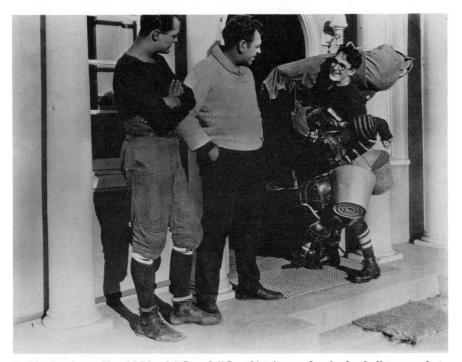

In *The Freshman* Harold Lloyd ("Speedy" Lamb) tries out for the football team only to wind up as a manager, still believing that he is a playing member of the varsity. Here, under the scrutiny of the team captain (James Anderson) and coach (Pat Harmon), Speedy cheerfully performs his managerial duties.

chance to play—mainly because most of the players have been injured, and the coach is forced to send him in. The surprising outcome, at least to the coach, the players, and those in the stands (but not to Speedy and the movie audience), is that, in spite of his unconventional play, Speedy manages to score the winning touchdown and become the admired hero he had always dreamed he could become. If there is a moral here, it no doubt stems from the film's suggestion that one's personal ideals can be stronger than any kind of system and that a determined belief in them can overcome the system in the end. At least, that is what the idealistic assumptions of the American way of life would have us believe.

The formula for a movie like *The Freshman* was not new, though. As early as *The Pinch Hitter* (Triangle, 1917), Charles Ray played a bumbling college athlete who is the butt of his classmates' jokes.[17] True to the expectations of this kind of movie, he somehow manages to win the big baseball game and become a hero in the eyes of his peers. In such a dramatic situation—the pattern of the innocent boldly confronting the system, being put down by it on occasion, yet winning out in the long run, no matter what the odds—we recognize something archetypal in the American experience. In *The Freshman,* Harold Lloyd's comic genius projected both the satirical and symbolic sides of the college-life obsession with social involvement to get at something deeper within the American ethos. His novel efforts would inspire and inform a number of collegiate films to follow.[18]

Although most critics considered it structurally weak, *College* (United Artists, 1927) was one of the more outstanding movies in the manner of *The Freshman,* due mainly to the performance of another of the all-time comedy greats. The most athletic of our silent comics, Buster Keaton vividly displayed his talent for dynamic physical expression in this film to color his version of what it was like to go to college in the 1920s. In contrast to the social acceptance that Lloyd's Speedy Lamb seeks from his fellow students, Keaton plays a studious college freshman named Ronald who wants to be liked by just one person, a co-ed named Mary with whom he is hopelessly in love. But Mary is more turned on by the advances of the college athletic hero than she is by the overtures of Ronald, who is not only bookish but antiathletic. Even so, Ronald finally gets the message that if he is ever to win over Mary, he'd better become a successful athlete. In fact, he goes so far as to try out for every sport offered at Clayton College, winding up a failure at each one—with the possible exception of rowing, since he unwittingly manages to urge his crew on to victory in this film's comic tour de force. But when Ronald discovers that his rival, in true villainous fashion, has locked Mary in a second-story room in order to carry out his own devious designs on her, he musters up a surprising store of superhuman energy to rescue his loved one from her fate. After a sensational sprint that transcribes to the screen as a world's record performance, Ronald effortlessly pole-vaults into the window of Mary's room to save her from her captor.[19] Whatever message may be intended here must be related to the understanding that the achievement of a goal or prize is only worthwhile when we find ourselves spurred on by real, human concerns and not by the artificial demands of a social system or an institution. However, the pessimistic posture of Buster Keaton, as it does in most of his films, seems to suggest another interpretation of Ronald and Mary's story.

Significantly, the real concerns of *College* grow out of the triangular relationship of its principals, another variation of a melodramatic convention that recurs in a multitude of films with a collegiate theme. As early as the 1914 Biograph film *Strongheart,* the collegiate ingredients of the triangular affair are found in what must have been a daring and unusual plot situation for its time. The story centers around an Indian student on the Columbia football team who is in love with a co-ed he courageously saved from drowning years before. The star of the team, the girl's present boy friend, is suspected of revealing team plays to an opponent, but the Indian (Strongheart) can't bear to see what this revelation will do to the girl he loves, so he

Buster Keaton's version of the college man in *College* (United Artists, 1927) was that of a misunderstood loner, as this still from the movie suggests.

takes the blame, thus enabling the star to play in the big game after all. When the truth comes out, though, social imperatives dictate that Strongheart be banished from college society for daring to love a white girl. While this film's lack of resolution disappointed most audiences, its dependence on the popular triangular relationship was evident from beginning to end.[20]

The triangular plot expressed itself in endless variations in the college-life film, but the theme of racial differences was quite rare.[21] A more representative, yet interesting, example of what was going on during this time was the sound film, *The Sophomore* (Pathé, 1929). Eddie Quillan plays a college athlete who, after losing his tuition money in a dice game, returns to his drugstore counter job, where waitress Sally O'Neill, his girl, learns of his plight. The third member of the triangle, the store manager, now enters the picture. Aware of the attraction between Sally and Eddie, he fires Eddie. Sally knows that the manager has a crush on her, and hits him for the tuition money. Eddie then returns to school and the football team while Sally tries to keep secret her bequest in his behalf, even going so far as to

A good example of the triangular plot on which many college-life movies were based was *Brown of Harvard* (MGM, 1926). Here, Francis X. Bushman collars William Haines for alienating him from Mary Brian.

enter Eddie's fraternity house to intercept her boss's telltale note. In the formulary tradition of the college-life film, this violation not only serves to alienate Eddie and Sally, it gets him kicked out of school right before the big game.

Then, in what is probably the most incredibly action-packed finale of any collegiate movie in the 1920s, Eddie is allowed to play, only to be knocked out and taken from the field. Upon discovering that Sally has been his benefactor, he catches up with her just as she is about to leave town on the train. After squaring things between them, Eddie then hustles back to the stadium right before the gun goes off—in time to tackle a teammate who had been running the wrong way and thus preserve a win. As ridiculous and absurd as its plot may sound, this film was popularly received, mainly because of its tongue-in-cheek approach to the clichés of the collegiate film, which by 1929 had become familiar fare to audiences.

If the demand for a more sophisticated interpretation of collegiate subject matter was becoming more evident by the late 1920s, the development of this attitude can be attributed in large part to a film like *College,* which apparently was the first collegiate movie to derive its overall satirical inspiration from the traditional clash between academia and athletics.[22] In high school Ronald, the hero of *College,* was an honor student whose graduation speech was called "The Curse of Athletics." Thus the dean of Clayton College assesses Ronald's academic ability and the dominance of sports with the remark: "A boy like you can make this athlete-infested college a seat of learning once more." But it does not take Ronald long to realize that the social demands of the collegiate system have elevated sports to a level of popular acceptance where the proficient athlete is more acclaimed and readily recognized than is the scholar. Trying to impress his girl and join the system, Ronald futilely attempts to beat the athletic hero at his own game, only to realize in the long run that it is through the simple virtues of sincerity and devotion, not the vainglorious accomplishments of the athletic field, that he can win Mary.

Of all the collegiate films produced during the 1920s, the silent classics, *College* and *The Freshman,* stand out as the prototypes for a large number of dramatic variations, extensions, and reactions that would follow in the years ahead. Even the startling, and to some viewers unnecessary, ending of *College,* which singles out the stereotyped moment of Ronald's personal triumph and contrasts it with life's ultimate indifference to individual achievement, seems to presage the satirical bite and critical venom of the collegiate films of the 1960s and 1970s.[23] (Two other influential types of collegiate film of the 1920s to which later movies would react are discussed in chapters 2 and 3: those based on military school life, and the popular series of Universal shorts known as *The Collegians* [Universal, 1926–29].)

By the end of the 1920s, the basic dramatic situation for the college-life movie—the personal ideals of the individual challenged by the realities of the collegiate social setting—had been sufficiently established to herald the next significant era of this kind of film and lead to many other variations of the genre, among them one of the most popular and appealing versions of the entire tradition: the all-singing, all-dancing, and all-talking musical of the 1930s.

2 Variations: The 1930s

At Siwash we always refused to carry books except when absolutely necessary. It seemed too affected—as if you were trying to learn something.

—George Fitch,
At Good Old Siwash (1911)

You gotta be a football hero
  to get along with the beautiful girls.
You gotta be a touchdown getter,
  you bet, if you wanna get a baby to pet.
—from "You Gotta Be a Football Hero"
by Al Sherman, Al Lewis, and Buddy Fields,
copyright 1933 by Leo Feist, Inc.

By the 1930s, the movies had come into their own not only as a cultural form but as a highly influential and dominant social force in the lives of the American people, as evidenced by moviegoers' attendance at theaters across the land. Even though the Depression years saw a falling off in weekly attendance, the dark days of this period prompted many people to continue going to the movies even when they could least afford to. Those who can still recall what it was like to view a film in either the neighborhood theaters or the great movie palaces of the time have probably discovered that their senses have long since been clouded over by the passage of time and the spell of nostalgia. As a result, those same films of the 1930s which we see today on television no longer convey the magic excitement and wide-ranging appeal that they did in those emotionally charged, semidark halls of another place, another time. Thus, many of us may find it difficult to be objective about an era that, in spite of its special problems, appears in retrospect to have been so remotely innocent. We can conclude, however, that the economic concerns of the Depression did contribute immeasurably to a Hollywood more sensitive than ever before or since to the escape wishes and fantasy needs of the moviegoing public. The result of this awareness was a veritable deluge of films fashioned to meet the masses' insatiable appetite for at least temporarily avoiding and/or fantasizing the problems of the workaday world. Accordingly, the college-life movie was only one of a number of popular film genres that developed along these lines during the 1930s, but the college-oriented film had its own unique approach to interpreting social experience, especially as it was expressed through the mode of musical comedy.

If college students of the 1930s were any more serious in their outlook than those of any other period, there is little film evidence to show for it, although they had a perfect right to a grim perspective, conditioned as they were by the lean, poverty-ridden Depression years. But the movies of that day stubbornly inform us that the era's students were experts at organizing extracurricular pursuits designed to fantasize the ascetic routine of their daily classroom activity. At least, that is what an abundance of film musicals of the time would have us believe. The truth is that films like *College Humor* (Paramount, 1933), *College Rhythm* (Paramount, 1934), and *College Swing* (Paramount 1938), in their all-out attempt to ignore the academic side of college life and avoid any reference to adverse conditions in the larger world, reveal a great deal about the escapist mood and fantasy obsessions of the American people at this time. Ironically, a similar mood of fantasy and escapism still pervades the country today, when even a higher standard of living has not made our personal problems any easier to bear. Thus, a film like *Animal House* (1978), although it makes the most of today's more liberal license to express the excesses of social behavior, is really not too far removed from the intent of a movie like *Horse Feathers* (1932) with its blatant disrespect for institutionalized behavior.

One of the unique characteristics about the students of the 1930s was that they represented the first generation to be inundated by a wave of popular culture images created by the mass-media forms of the movies, radio, magazines, and the recording industry. Although these modes of popular expression had succeeded in promoting a large number of public images for mass adulation in the 1920s, the climate for the appeasement of the nation's fantasy hunger was more conducive to this sort of thing in the 1930s, when an interrelationship of mutual inspiration began to spring up among the media, finding its central focus in the movies. Rising young stars of radio like Bob

This ad for Paramount's *College Holiday* (1936) typifies the fantasized approach to life that college-life musicals of the 1930s projected.

Hope, Jack Benny, and the George Burns–Gracie Allen team, for example, all appeared in college-life movies during the 1930s. In fact, the singing professor of *College Humor* was played by a young crooner named Bing Crosby who proved in this film that he could act as well as sing.

Because it represented the most direct access to fantasy and escape, the Hollywood musical—a vehicle that depended more on spectacular stage settings and exotic trappings for dramatic effect than on its story—was among the dominant film forms of the 1930s. Early movie musicals were usually nothing more than direct transplants of their stage versions, and many films unfortunately made the mistake of carrying over into the more expansive medium of film the static conditions of the stage, thus missing out on some rich opportunities to embellish upon their Broadway counterparts. When a visually oriented director like Busby Berkeley demonstrated the limitless potential of the musical in films like *Footlight Parade* and *42nd Street,* he established a movie technique which not only dominated the 1930s but influenced the entire Hollywood musical tradition. Especially sensitive to the fantasy moods of his audience, Berkeley purposely neglected the pedestrian concerns of plot to create grandiose and elaborate sets on which an eye-popping display of beautiful show girls cavorted in mind-boggling song and dance routines. Berkeley intuitively realized that by pleasing both the eye and ear with exotic variations of the song-and-dance performance, the movie musical could easily mask any deficiency in story line.

It was only natural, then, that during the 1930s a highly romanticized view of college life competed with a fantasized New York City as the most popular settings to stage the conventions of the Hollywood musical. Judging from the overwhelming number that was turned out, it appears that the musical was the most influential form of collegiate film to condition the popular conception of what it might be like to go to an attractively remote place like college. The films of the silent era may have established the basic formula and contributed to the social atmosphere and tone of the college-life movie, but it was the sparkling, happy-go-lucky musical of the 1930s that caught the perfect blend of youthful exuberance and social involvement to create a special kind of fantasized experience that captivated many moviegoers of the era.

With the development of sound approaching technical perfection, 1929 saw the appearance of four key college-life films that were among the first musical movies: *The Forward Pass* (First National), *So This Is College* (MGM), *Words and Music* (Fox), and *Sweetie* (Paramount). Although they depended a great deal on the standard clichés of the 1920s collegiate movie, these films all received favorable reviews—mainly because of the novelty of the musical movie at this time. In retrospect, though, the underlying significance of these films is that each one is built around a basic plot ingredient that would recur in all the college-life musicals to follow: the big game convention, the triangular plot, the big show scheme, and the college inheritance theme.[1] However, it was the enhancement of film through sound, not the variations of plot, that gave audiences an exciting new dimension to their moviegoing experience.

Because sound quality itself had become an integral part of a movie, film critics of the day began to consider its quality as an important feature of their reviews. For example, in 1928 when Paramount made a college love story starring Buddy Rogers and Mary Brian called *Varsity* and utilized only thirteen minutes of dialogue, a critic panned the film as lacking box office attractiveness."[2] On the other hand, *So This Is College* was praised for its contribution to the experimental and realistic use of sound during its football and musical sequences, as the following excerpt from a contemporary review points out:

Recording and camera work [are] of the best, and especially during the game. Mikes have evidently picked up the mixture of screams and yells from the USC side of the LA Bowl so truly as to make an

The fraternity high jinks of one of the first college-life musicals, *So This Is College* (MGM, 1929), were much more subdued than those of *Animal House*, some fifty years later. Robert Montgomery glowers at the clowning of Elliott Nugent while Cliff Edwards, atop the piano, strums a real ukelele.

audience tingle. . . . Feature also marks one of the few instances of a studio taking the theatrical license to imply an off-screen orchestra accompaniment without manufacturing an excuse.[3]

Hollywood, in learning how to use sound to good advantage, was also learning how to put together visually exciting, highly entertaining musicals. In 1930, Metro-Goldwyn-Mayer demonstrated its special approach to the musical form when it brought out the first film version of *Good News,* a collegiate musical based on the 1927 Broadway hit. Featuring the comedic talents of Bessie Love and Gus Shy, the film highlighted the popular production numbers of the stage version in such a way that they not only justified the relegation of plot to a secondary function but also helped single out Metro-Goldwyn-Mayer as an up-and-coming studio for the production of the Hollywood musical.[4]

But it was Paramount that was the pace setter in the field of college-life musicals at this time. Because of one of its film's transitional significance in which the influences of vaudeville, the stage musical, and the conventions of the college-life film all come together, we need to turn our attention here to Paramount's most representative film in this genre—*Horse Feathers* (1932). As the prime target of the Marx Brothers—evidenced by the merciless cracks of Groucho, the supporting shenanigans of Chico and Harpo, and even the comparatively straight role of Zeppo—the venerable institution of the American college was put on the defensive right at the outset of this film. In fact, two major components of academic organization and extracurricular activity are lampooned throughout this movie: the establishment, particularly the board of trustees and the administration, and the system of big-time football.

Like most Americans of the 1930s, the Marxes looked upon the academic formality and ivory-tower isolation of higher education as an alien experience. Self-made and hardened to the cultural subtleties of the finer things that the college education extolled, the Brothers' comedic style, liberally spiced with Groucho and Chico's outrageous wisecracking and punning, emanated from their special understanding of a social conflict between what one has learned from experience and what one is supposed to have learned from books and the system of formal education. At one point in *Horse Feathers,* for example, Groucho underscores the pomposity of the academic stance when he takes over a classroom and proceeds to "enlighten" his students with a running commentary of his unique brand of knowledge, which consists of a series of absurd observations offset by the slapstick antics of Chico and Harpo, who happen to be seated among the students. Typically, when Groucho admonishes Harpo that it will be more difficult for him to burn the candle at both ends as he grows older, Harpo merely grins and reaches under his trenchcoat to procure— what else?—a candle burning at both ends! Such carryings-on were in the direct tradition of the vaudeville theater, and Groucho's crackpot professor routine was only one of many vivid examples of what he and his brothers had inherited from this tradition. Through the Marx Brothers' satirical put-down of our system of higher education, we see their peculiar understanding of the collegiate experience, like that of Hollywood's, as a conflict between social reality and the high expectations of American idealism.

As Quincy Adams Wagstaff, the newly appointed president of Huxley College, Groucho himself expresses at the beginning of the film the pecking-order relationship and bureaucratic hypocrisy that any kind of administrative hierarchy always seems dependent on. When he voices his new presidential policies in the Gilbert-and-Sullivan-type patter song, "I'm Against It," his bearded professors, all dressed in academic regalia, jump in unison to echo his position. Ironically, one of the most popular conventions of the stage musi-

Biology professor Robert Craig falls prey to the anti-intellectual barbs of Groucho Marx in *Horse Feathers* (Paramount, 1932).

cal—the full ensemble production—is utilized here to suggest the parrotlike behavior of those caught up in the group demands of a complex social system. Whatever it is that President Wagstaff is against, the professors gyrate and gesture that they're against it, too. But because the school hasn't had a winning football team since 1888, Groucho makes it clear to his staff that he is surely for one thing—a winning football team. In fact, the basic plot of *Horse Feathers* deals with Huxley's attempt to recruit two star players in order to win the big game with Darwin. Huxley's opponents, however, have already recruited the same two athletes that Groucho wants. While visiting a local speakeasy where the players are supposed to hang out, Groucho mistakes Chico and Harpo as his potential stars, signs them up instead, and thus sets the stage for one of the wildest football sequences ever filmed.

Even though a more sophisticated attitude may have developed toward intercollegiate football since the time of *Horse Feathers*, it is a credit to the underlying perceptiveness of this film that much of it still rings true today regarding the abuses and inordinate demands of big-time college sports. One of the more telling and pungent lines in the movie is Groucho's admonishment of two professors that, "we're neglecting football for education," to which the lackey profs agree, only to have Groucho suddenly change his mind and force the academicians to change theirs as well. Thus, the major subject of *Horse Feathers* is football, around which all the film's lampooning of our system of higher education revolves. The climax of the movie, of course, is the big game with bitter rival Darwin, an episode which in itself comes across as a spoof of the collegiate movie convention that makes such an event obligatory to plot development. In overcoming the predictable roadblocks that have been perpetrated to keep them from participating in and possibly winning the game, Chico and Harpo finally join forces with Groucho, and after trailing 12–0 at the half, come up with a style of play based on their own rules, and produce a triple-threat punch that the Darwinites find impossible to stave off. Actually, the boys not only go on to win the game, but in true collegiate film fashion they also win the girl, college-widow-type Thelma Todd. The film ends in typical Marx madness, with Groucho, Chico, and Harpo all marrying Miss Todd, a conclusion so absurd that it has to rate as the ultimate put-down of the cliché ending where the guy always gets the girl. *Horse Feathers,* whose overall humorous effect was due in large part to S. J. Perelman's contribution to its script, may have occasionally gotten sidetracked, but it still stands as one of the finest examples of a film in which both the collegiate system and the college-life film genre itself come in for equal shares of ridicule.

The iconoclastic bite of *Horse Feathers* went largely unappreciated in the 1930s in favor of this film's periodic flights of fancy, which moviegoers of that troubled era must have found more attractive than any kind of social criticism. Nonetheless, *Horse Feathers* is a landmark film in the college-life tradition, mainly because of its skillful blending of the ingredients of satire, the collegiate romance, occasional musical interludes, and the big game build-up—all basic elements of the college-life musicals and films that followed. In an era when movies on the order of the Universal horror classics and the Warner Brothers crime films were extremely popular, it became clear that the Hollywood conception of the collegiate experience also permitted a fantasized approach to life. Because this interpretation of the collegiate life-style was so adaptable to the conventions of the Hollywood musical, a voluminous number of them appeared from 1933 to 1939, probably Hollywood's richest period for transcribing its dream fantasies onto the silver screen. While many of these films may best be forgotten, a number of them are significant and interesting not only because they mirrored the day's popular tastes but because they existed as vehicles for the special talents of both the established and the budding stars of radio, records, and film. Mercifully, many of these hopefuls faded with the movies they appeared in, but some of the best fortunately went on to greater stardom: Jack Oakie, Betty Grable, Dick Powell, Judy Garland, and, of course, Bing Crosby.

Harry Lillis Crosby (1904–77), one of the most versatile performers in entertainment history, first began to display his unique talents in the collegiate films of the 1930s. Because of his singing prowess, he had appeared briefly in a musical called *King of Jazz* (Universal, 1930) and a 1931 Paramount college-life film, *Confessions of a Co-ed*. In *College Humor* (Paramount, 1933), his second starring role after *The Big Broadcast* (Paramount, 1932), he came into his own as a natural entertainer, and spirited this picture to one of the bigger box office draws of the time. In playing a collegiate movie role, Crosby had real-life qualifications stemming from a short stint at Gonzaga University in his native Tacoma—an experience he undoubtedly drew on to enhance the naturalness of his acting. But over the years nearly all of Bing Crosby's performances came to be appreciated by his fans for their easygoing, down-to-earth manner. This personal trademark ultimately attracted thousands of moviegoers to his films.

Crooning and spooning are a big part of professor Bing Crosby's lesson plans for co-ed Mary Carlisle in *College Humor* (Paramount, 1933).

Characteristically, in *College Humor* Bing is cast as a swinging college professor at a midwestern school where he woos one of the prettier college belles (Mary Carlisle) away from the football star (Richard Arlen). Incredibly, but typically, the plot calls for Professor Crosby to relate to his students in the classroom as a "crooner," a then popular term for a male singer of romantic ballads. Actually, this kind of role derived from Bing's growing radio appeal, for that medium had begun to have considerable influence on the moviemakers of the 1930s. Accordingly, George Burns and Gracie Allen, then at the beginning of their radio popularity, put in a brief appearance in a comedy routine, but it is the Crosby charisma and its contribution to tunes like "Learn to Croon" that steal the show. A slender Jack Oakie lends laughs to the main story line and, as a football player, functions as a key figure in the conventional big game finale of this film. In spite of the film's dependence on the genre clichés of the triangular plot, the campus show, and the big game wind-up, a contemporary reviewer observes that because *College Humor* affects a lampoon manner, these familiar ingredients "aren't so hard to take."[5] Casting Bing Crosby in an academic role was a positive move in that it helped counteract the public's generally negative image of professors—an attitude we observe fluctuating throughout the 1930s version of the college-life tradition.

The following year found the increasingly popular Crosby cast in another college-life musical, *She Loves Me Not* (Paramount, 1934), a picture with a lot more meat on the story line than any in which he had previously appeared. Based on the popular play by Howard Lindsay, this film allowed the talented Crosby to show off more than just his ability to handle hit songs like "Love in Bloom"; it uncovered his natural comedic ability that was to shine in so many films to follow. Designed in the manner of the screwball comedy that was so popular in the 1930s, *She Loves Me Not* takes place on a Hollywood version of the Princeton campus where Bing and his roommate (Edward Nugent) harbor a young woman (Miriam Hopkins) who has witnessed a murder and is therefore fearful of retribution. Since the administration forbids women in men's dormitories (a situation in itself quite laughable today), they dress her as a man, a predicament which precipitates several amusing turns of plot, even contributing to Bing's breakup with his regular girl friend (Kitty Carlisle). Although the film's neatly structured plot raises it well above the standards of the usual collegiate movie, *She Loves Me Not* holds true to the genre's antiestablishment tradition by setting up the college administration to take the brunt of comic ridicule while the students, particularly Crosby and Nugent, come through as highly personable and well-meaning individuals who manage to beat the system. Even though Crosby himself did not make another college-life film until

High Time (20th Century-Fox, 1960), *She Loves Me Not* was remade in 1955 as *How to Be Very, Very Popular,* starring one of the all-time collegiate film performers, Betty Grable.

Betty, who was born in 1916 and broke into the movies while still in her teens in 1930, was the co-ed counterpart of Jack Oakie's football player, and like Oakie she appeared in just about every variation of the college-life movie that scriptwriters could come up with. While not very polished as an actress, she could sing and dance creditably, and for most moviegoers of the 1930s these were impressive enough talents for a popular mòvie starlet. However, Betty's real redeeming grace was what has been referred to as the all-American girl's fresh, wholesome look—a quality that undoubtedly impressed the movie people in their attempt to capture on film their version of the college-girl image of the time. In fact, the co-ed type that Betty Grable portrayed was a distinct reaction to the uninhibited life-style of a Clara Bow, but it unfortunately did very little for her acting career. Destined for better things in the colorful Fox musicals of the 1940s, Betty in the meantime must have set a record with her number of appearances in collegiate films during the 1930s. At first, most of them were rather innocuous features like Monogram's *The Sweetheart of Sigma Chi* (1933), MGM's *Student Tour* (1934), and RKO's *Old Man Rhythm* (1935).[6]

Obviously, Betty's appealing demeanor and ingratiating manner contributed a great deal toward typecasting her as Hollywood's co-ed queen, and 1936 saw her appearing in two of the better college-oriented musicals—*Pigskin Parade* (20th Century-Fox) and *Collegiate* (Paramount). The plot of the former film offered a unique twist to the standard football caper by having a Texas cow college come East to play against Yale, then a national gridiron power. It seems that the Yalies had originally elected to play the University of Texas, but through a scheduling oversight instead play a school that no one has ever heard of—"Texas State University." The game shapes up as a complete mismatch until the coach of the Texas team (Jack Haley) discovers a farm boy (Stu Erwin) who can throw a muskmelon a country mile. When Coach Haley signs up Erwin and has him direct his special talent toward throwing a football, the results are devastating for the Yale Bulldogs in this entertaining expression of the collegiate's film's favorite theme: confronting and overcoming the social imperatives of a sophisticated system through a naturally innocent approach.

Another noteworthy point about *Pigskin Parade* is that it was the first feature film for Judy Garland, then only fourteen years old. Judy plays Stu Erwin's country bumpkin sister, whose talent for singing, which the critics were quick to spot, adds a special dimension to the film. In the meantime, Betty Grable is relegated to the role of Stu

Long-time movie fans remember Betty Grable as a swinging, singing hoofer in her co-ed roles. Here, in *College Swing* (Paramount, 1938), she steps out with new husband Jackie Coogan (left). They're backed up by Skinnay Ennis and his band.

Erwin's girl friend, and as usual comes across as just another pretty face.

Collegiate was Betty's first film for Paramount, the studio whose output topped all college-life movie producers at this time. It saw her cast with Jack Oakie, who instead of performing in his usual role as a football player, comes on as a playboy type who inherits a girls' school and discovers that he is to be its dean. Dean Oakie decides that a singing and dancing curriculum should be the order of the day—certainly the perfect excuse to organize musical productions of the Hollywood variety, as well as an obvious example of Hollywood's escapist reaction to the deeper concerns and issues of the time. Based on *The Charm School* by Alice Duer Miller, *Collegiate* was unique in having the composers of the film's score, Mack Gordon and Harry Revel, playing themselves as cochairmen of the school's music department. They, of course, find themselves unusually busy in the kind of school Oakie has set up. Like most of the girls in attendance, though, Miss Grable finds herself functioning in a merely decorative role. More challenging parts lay just ahead.

Jack Oakie (1903–78), who appeared with Betty Grable in several collegiate films, is a significant figure in the development of this genre if only because of his numerous roles as a college football player. Possessed of an amiable, rough-hewn physical appearance, Oakie undoubtedly fitted the description that most casting directors of the 1930s imagined for a football player. Despite this typecasting, Oakie as an actor was surprisingly flexible. Whereas he had offset star athlete Richard Arlen in *College Humor* and dominated the slight dramatic action of *Collegiate,* he effectively counteracted the image of singer Lanny Ross in *College Rhythm* (Paramount, 1934). The story line in this film is inspired by a rivalry between Oakie and Ross that extends from the football field to the business world after graduation. This situation makes for a novel twist as collegiate publicity tactics are relied on to perk up the sales of a faltering department store, while the plot is periodically broken up with musical interludes by Ross and comedy spots by popular radio comic Joe ("Wanna buy a duck?") Penner. Mary Brian and Helen Mack supply the feminine romantic interest, and of course Oakie plays his usual opinionated football player, a role that one reviewer said he could "play in his sleep by now."[7]

"Collegians" Jack Oakie, Frances Langford, and Joe Penner tried to look as young as the camera would allow in *Collegiate* (Paramount, 1936).

Oakie, whose college-life film career dated from *The Wild Party* and *Sweetie* in 1929, would make other collegiate movie appearances on into the 1940s. Whether playing a wiseacre or a dumb ox, he seemed able to take on all his roles with considerable aplomb, but undoubtedly he owed a great deal of his success to his innate ability to capitalize on Hollywood's interpretation of athletics as a form of show business. Accordingly, the familiar role of a Jack Oakie type was projected in countless versions of the collegiate movie when the big-game finale was held in suspense due to any one of a variety of problems involving the team's star player: being placed on academic probation, attempting to throw the game through gambling connections, being kidnapped by gamblers or supporters of the rival team, becoming ill and being confined to the infirmary, and, of course, enduring romantic conflicts with stubborn girl friends.[8]

In the 1930s, radio was approaching the peak of its popularity, mainly because of personalities like *College Rhythm*'s Joe Penner and Lanny Ross, who were being actively promoted. The movies, ever sensitive to changes in public taste, moved fast to capitalize on the visual aspects of this phenomenon. The college-life movie in particular proved a favorite vehicle for this development, since it was designed primarily for a youth-oriented audience much given to the latest social preoccupations and pop-culture fads. Typical of the movie makers' sensitivity to the latest fads was *College Swing* (Paramount, 1938) in which Betty Grable and her newly acquired husband Jackie Coogan engage in a disconnected series of campus escapades with the likes of radio performers George Burns and Gracie Allen, Martha Raye, Jerry Colonna, and Bob Hope—all relative newcomers to the movie screen.

The inheritance theme was common during the economically depressed 1930s, and *College Swing*'s plot once again attested to the popularity of the comic situation where a character inherits a college and then must decide what to do with it. Heiress Gracie Allen, in her usual scatterbrained manner, comes up with the idea of transforming her school into a swinging campus where ex-vaudeville stars are appointed as ranking professors! No doubt this innovative approach was designed to pump some new life into a tired plot situation, but unfortunately this variation comes across as nothing more than a staged series of variety acts where, in true vaudeville fashion, the featured performers get a chance to do their thing. Ironically, Miss Grable, finally lands a part of some substance as a college flirt, but without much of a plot to back her up, her role seems rather pointless. Although *College Swing* was Betty Grable's last musical of the 1930s, she did appear in other types of college-life films which will be discussed later in this section.

Originally founded by Adolph Zukor as the Famous Players

studios, Paramount Pictures Corporation placed its emphasis at this time on entertainment fare that offered something for the entire family. It was the natural choice for producing musicals in which the plot, what there was of it, revolved around the romantic comedy caprices of co-ed Betty Grable, since these concerns never seemed to be so serious that they couldn't be easily resolved. Collegiate films of the Paramount stripe clearly revealed that their version of college life, particularly as it was musically perceived, consisted of a purely make-believe nonintellectual atmosphere where the most profound problems were winning the big game that puts the school on the map, or staging a campus show to raise enough money to keep the school solvent.

One of Paramount's more unusual approaches to fantasizing the collegiate experience was *College Holiday* (1936), a musical with one of the most bizarre plots ever devised by a Hollywood scriptwriter. In this one, Jack Benny, another leading radio entertainer of the time, plays the role of a hotel manager who is prevailed upon by a eugenics theorist (Mary Boland) to bring together a mixed group of college students at Benny's hotel to conduct an experiment designed to find out whether students from particular ethnic backgrounds are smarter than others. Evidently, this could be a touchy civil rights concern even at this time, since Benny addresses the audience at the movie's close with what amounts to a disclaimer, saying that everything has been in good fun and that he hopes everyone has enjoyed it all. Outside of Benny's wry wit, most of *College Holiday*'s "fun" consists of the comedy routines of George Burns and Gracie Allen intermingled with the misadventures of Martha Raye and Ben Blue. Incidentally, a youthful Johnny Downs, who will show up in many another collegiate movie, performs as a dancer, and Benny's comic image link with the popular tune "Love in Bloom" begins with this film.

Other studios turned out collegiate musicals at this time, but had difficulty in matching the popularity of even Paramount's weakest efforts. In 1935, the Fox studios attempted a muscial of John Erskine's well-received novel *Bachelor of Arts,* only to see it wind up as the second feature of a double bill in most movie houses. In *Freshman Love* (1936), Warner Brothers dusted off the college-widow theme of the silent era, but the plot of this film was so predictable that even the mediocre musical interludes came as a welcome relief. In 1937, Warner Brothers produced *Over the Goal,* another "pigskin opry," as a *Variety* reviewer referred to it. Headlined by June Travis, this film featured a cast of relative unknowns—unless audiences considered the 1937 Southern California football team as noteworthy actors.[9]

The year 1938 saw some improvement. Twentieth Century-Fox carried on the popular Hollywood tradition of spotlighting a popular athletic personality by casting Olympic ice-skating champion Sonja Henie in a collegiate musical called *My Lucky Star*. In this, her fourth Hollywood movie, the petite Norwegian blonde becomes involved in a large department store's publicity stunt to advertise its winter sportswear when she is sent to perform in an ice carnival at a New England college modeled after Dartmouth. Designed primarily to show off Miss Henie's talents on the ice, *My Lucky Star* had Richard Greene and Cesar Romero as the men in her life, while Joan Davis, Buddy Ebsen, and Arthur Treacher lent the film solid comedy support. Once again, champion collegiate song composers Mack Gordon and Harry Revel collaborated on a popularly pleasing score.

Also in 1938, Columbia got on the collegiate bandwagon with one of the better low-budget musicals, *Start Cheering,* in which Jimmy Durante displays his outstanding comedy talent in the role of a wacky actors' agent whose leading star, Charles Starrett, decides to forego his promising career to get a college education. The plot develops around the schemes of Durante and his boss Walter Connolly to get their protégé kicked out of school. When Starrett tries out for the football team, the players, led by Broderick Crawford (a recent star in the Broadway success *Of Mice and Men*), help discourage his efforts by giving him a working over every chance they get. It seems that Crawford and the other players don't go for the way the handsome Starrett gets along with the co-eds. True to the tradition of Harold Lloyd's role in *The Freshman,* however, *Start Cheering* is another example of the long-suffering hero who overcomes his special problems in the end.[10]

Not to be outdone by the other studios, Universal brought forth its version of the college-life musical in 1938, but *Freshman Year* was unique in the one respect of substituting a campus show climax for the football finale. When star William Lundigan comes up with the idea of selling "flunk insurance" to his fellow students at fifty cents a policy, his scheme is scuttled as one of the professors, after being criticized in the school newspaper, retaliates by handing out failing grades to nearly all the freshmen. Lundigan's only hope to get himself out of hock, it seems, is to organize and promote a big, crowd-pleasing collegiate review—really a convenient pretext for presenting the stage and radio stars who were signed for this film.

The college-life musicals of 1938—*My Lucky Star, Start Cheering,* and *Freshman Year*—may have been a notch or two above their predecessors in overall quality, but they still failed to project that pervasive aura of good feeling that the Paramount studios seemed to work with so well. Undoubtedly, audiences of the 1930s found the Paramount view of the social side of college life most agreeable and entertaining.

Ironically, the period's biggest high quality musical film inspired by the collegiate vogue was Warner Brothers' *Varsity Show* (1937), starring Dick Powell, the Warner lot's answer to Bing Crosby. Powell (1904–63) would eventually exchange his crooner's image for that of a cool-talking tough guy in the 1940s, but during the 1930s his name featured in a musical comedy helped attract customers to theaters all across the country. At two hours, *Varsity Show* was among the longest movie musicals of its day, and the fact that the innovative Busby Berkeley directed the production numbers of this film must have had something to do with both its length and quality. Widely renowned by this time for his spectacular staging effects and experimental camera work, Berkeley brought this movie to a close with one of his most impressive and unforgettable settings—a huge staircase over which several hundred young men and women in collegiate dress swarm to create formations representative of the schools they are saluting. The overall effect was the biggest and most grandiose job of recruiting that these educational institutions had ever received at any one time, and college public relations people must have fairly drooled when they first saw this production.

Varsity Show's story is based on the stock situation of Winfield College's desperate need for professional help in putting on its annual

Dick Powell braves the paddle line in *Varsity Show* (Warner Bros., 1937), the period's collegiate musical blockbuster.

show. A special twist of the plot has the students obtaining the services of Winfield alumnus Powell, now a famous Broadway producer who has fallen on hard times. After much persuading on the part of the collegians, Powell takes on the assignment, and things begin to pick up for him, particularly his love life, which finds its inspiration in the vivacious and energetic Rosemary Lane. By the smashing finale, which even outdoes this movie's staging of nine catchy tunes by Richard Whiting and Johnny Mercer, things appear to have worked out for everyone in the film as well as for the college public relations folks.

A significant sidelight to the casting of *Varsity Show,* yet one pertinent to this study, is the choice of two distinctly contrasting professorial types: Fred Waring (director of the popular radio singing ensemble The Pennsylvanians) as an amiable professor of music; and Walter Catlett as Professor Sylvester Biddle, the crotchety character that most American audiences were conditioned to expect in the role of an academician. The striking difference between the behavior of Waring and that of Catlett points out the ambivalence that existed in both the movies' posture and the public's mind toward the image of the college professor at this time. This ambivalence was most sharply revealed in *Horse Feathers* in the college president role of Groucho Marx, who is an integral part of the system at the same time that he is poking fun at it. For comic effect, most roles for academic types were decidedly negative, as in the case of Charles Butterworth in *Student Tour* and, of course, Walter Catlett in *Varsity Show,* although some characters, like Bing Crosby's in *College Humor* and Fred Waring's in *Varsity Show,* were positively depicted as popular, well-meaning professors who are up on the latest fads and obviously interested in the same things their students are. One of the more interesting variations of this interpretation was portrayed by Pinky Tomlin in a sleeper film called *Swing It, Professor* (Ambassador, 1938). Tomlin plays a college music teacher who detests swing music but is eventually won over to its cause, much to the delight of audiences who viewed Tomlin's ingratiating performance. Most moviegoers during the 1930s liked college professors who turned out to be regular guys, it seems.[11]

In many of the early collegiate films, the professor had been ignored altogether. When he does start to show up with some frequency in the 1930s, it is either as a congenial, personable type or, more often, as a crackpot. This wide divergence of characterization, which ranges from the appealing to the downgrading, points out the movies' receptivity to sudden shifts in the public's social attitudes. However, negative stereotyping of the professorial role continued on into the 1960s when it found its ultimate expression in the Jerry Lewis lead in *The Nutty Professor* (Paramount, 1963). His was a reverse

Jekyll-Hyde interpretation whose comedic effect was derived from a bumbling, scholarly recluse's attempt to make himself over into a winning personality (see chapter 4). Not until the intensely social-conscious films of recent years would the college professor step forth as a full-blown character—for example, in the forceful role played by John Houseman in 1973's *The Paper Chase* (see chapter 4).

For all Hollywood studios, the decade of the 1930s was the most popular period for the college-life film. A significant factor contributing to this success was the growing popularity of intercollegiate football. *Liberty* magazine for 1 October 1938, reported college football as a $50 million a year business, an astronomical sum during the Depression.[12] A major reason for this expanding interest was that the game of football, especially as it was played by our collegians, had been around long enough for it to have created its own kind of mythology—a special type of mystique that we will encounter from time to time throughout this book, particularly in my assessment of the movies that take the game of football seriously.

Interestingly enough, though, there were a couple of musically oriented films of the late 1930s that pulled out all the stops to poke fun at the game. One of them was a Ritz Brothers vehicle with a title that ironically bears out the idealistic side of the collegiate experience— *Life Begins in College* (20th Century-Fox, 1937). The Ritz Brothers— Al, Jim, and Harry—were never as big as the Marxes, of course, but this film stands as probably the best of the four they made in their peak year of 1937 and helped establish their popularity with moviegoers of the day. Because of the Ritzes' nightclub background, their films were designed to emphasize their knockabout routines through a series of madcap comedy antics. Consequently, *Life Begins in College,* which is structured and paced according to the brothers' zany, slapstick brand of comedy, has them participating in everything from football to a rhumba specialty. Other players—Joan Davis, Gloria Stuart, Tony Martin (who is around long enough to deliver one song), and Nat Pendleton as an Indian football star—add just enough variety not to detract from the comedy team at center stage. Because this film recognized the typical collegiate movie hokum for what it is, it served as a needed counterbalance and a refreshing interlude during a period in which college football grew into a mass obsession.

The other musical satirizing the football compulsion was also turned out by 20th Century-Fox. *Hold That Co-ed* (1938) is a perceptive lampoon of the politician motivated to make his down-and-out state university a nationally recognized football power. In director George Marshall's skillful handling of the elements of satire, a highly entertaining blend of political buffoonery and football high jinks is created. John Barrymore, as a governor molded in the tradition of Louisiana's Huey Long, manages to steal the show away from another featured performer, George Murphy, who would eventually become a politician in his own right. Murphy's role, when he's not too busy dancing, is as a coach of the team that Barrymore, through various political machinations for money and support, hopes to transform into a gridiron power. An unusual feminist slant to the story, one long before its time, has comedienne Joan Davis performing as a football player whose inspired attempts to score the winning touchdown against a wind of hurricane force not only exhibit her comic talent but add to the suspense surrounding the game's outcome and the film's climax. Not since *Horse Feathers* had the forces affecting the system of American higher education been lampooned so hilariously and pointedly as they were in this film, particularly those high-powered promotional schemes patently designed to put a school on the map.[13]

While intercollegiate football was the target of the wild humor of *Life Begins in College* and *Hold That Co-ed,* many another collegiate movie of the 1930s held firmly to the notion that the game of football was pretty serious business. Starting in the 1920s with dramas like *The Quarterback* and *One Minute to Play,* football was nearly always utilized in serious collegiate films to get across a moral lesson, function as a test of manhood, or contribute to character development. Something about the nature of the game seemed dramatically right for the movies, especially that part of the standard scenario which concerned itself with the personal conflicts of the gridiron gladiators themselves as they trained religiously to perform in the giant stadiums of big-time college football. As it was melodramatically interpreted by the movies of the 1930s, football was a game with a code of honor that could command a player to get out of a sick bed, hobble on to the field with a minute left to play, and come through with the big play that would win the game for good old Siwash. The heroic act that tests an individual's manliness and courage in the face of adversity was a plot convention echoed in the prolific and ubiquitous pulp magazines as well as some of the leading slick journals of the period, which devoted a significant amount of space to short stories and novelettes dealing with college football. With the image so well established both in fiction and in real life, it merely remained for Hollywood to draw upon what had already been tested as tried-and-true material for mass entertainment. It was the movies, then, more than any other creative form, that extended the variations of the football story to the absolute dramatic limit. Sometimes, though, real life furnished material that challenged both fiction and the movies, as was the case with the playing career of all-American Red Grange and the legendary coaching achievements of Knute Rockne of Notre Dame.

As a paradoxical composite of inspirational genius, brilliant tactician, and hard-sell huckster, Knute Rockne (1888–1931) was the

In *Hold That Co-ed* (20th Century-Fox, 1938), top-hatted governor John Barrymore takes enough interest in the fortunes of his state university's football team to sit on the bench with his coach (George Murphy) and players: Guinn Williams and Joan Davis, who apparently was before her time in championing women's rights in athletics.

kind of dynamic personality whom the movie people recognized right away as a natural for translation to the movie screen. Sensing the box-office potential for a movie about this fabulous coach who died tragically in a plane crash in 1931, Universal brought out *The Spirit of Notre Dame* in the same year. Starring Lew Ayres, Andy Devine, and J. Farrell McDonald as Rockne, this film was notable for its use of real-life players, including the much-publicized Notre Dame backfield that sports writer Grantland Rice had dubbed "the Four Horsemen." But the main quality that stood out in this movie was its dramatization of the indomitable Rockne charisma, which inspired and defined a special mystique that still permeates the spirit of college football.

Rockne's story is that of the American self-made man who capitalized on every opportunity which came his way to get ahead. At Notre Dame he had been a superior student and a hard-nosed football player himself. He had helped revolutionize the game in 1913 when he and teammate Gus Dorais demonstrated what could be done with the then little-used forward pass to demolish a highly respected Army team. Becoming head coach of his alma mater in 1918, Rockne went on to win 105 games and lose only twelve, while five of his teams went unbeaten. Most of Rockne's tremendous coaching success was attributable to his uncanny ability to get the most out of his players, and as if to emphasize the strong and pervasive personal influence Rockne wielded over his players, *The Spirit of Notre Dame*'s plot turns on the situation of an estranged relationship between two star players (Ayres and William Bakewell) who are college roommates. The object lesson of the film is brought out in the way Coach Rockne handles the touchy situation that has developed between his two highly prized athletes. Naturally, it is Rockne's psychological insight into human relationships that pays off in the end as Ayres and Bakewell are encouraged to resolve their differences in time to win the big game. The image of the college football coach had been growing in public esteem since the 1920s, and a movie like *The Spirit of Notre Dame* served to enhance the almost religious fervor surrounding the figure of the coach. In fact, many of the scenes in this film are so idealized with respect to the coaching genius and philosophy of Knute Rockne that the players who are a part of his system come across as controlled puppets who never seem to get their uniforms dirty. Ironically, the parade of real-life football stars like Frank Carideo, Don Miller, and Elmer Layden, instead of lending authenticity to the story, contributed both to the artificiality of the dramatic action and to the growing mass attitude that sports could be considered as pure entertainment—an outlook still very much with us.[14]

In marked contrast to the Rockne film, another 1931 movie—Columbia's *Maker of Men*—depended on a bitter clash between a coach and his player son as the basis for its plot. The son (Richard Cromwell) is compelled to quit the team coached by his father (Jack Holt) and enroll in another school because of his cowardly behavior on the gridiron. Apparently the change works out well for Cromwell, who finally begins to understand his father's intense dedication to the game. *Maker of Men* is another film that attempts to show how football can influence character development, but the ironic ending in which the son plays against his father's team and defeats it singlehandedly fails to come off in the proper dramatic sense. *Maker of Men* actually reflects Hollywood's straining after a unique plot variation in a highly overworked mode.[15]

One individual who not only contributed a great deal to the Hollywood version of the collegiate football movie but also unwittingly helped to demythologize the athlete in the movies was the versatile Francis Wallace. A graduate of Notre Dame, Wallace was a prolific writer who turned out works that ranged from popular fiction and nonfiction to screenplays, many of which were inspired by the legendary achievements of the intercollegiate football program at Notre

Look-alike J. Farrell McDonald turned in a convincing performance as Notre Dame coach Knute Rockne in *The Spirit of Notre Dame* (Universal, 1931). Here, he confronts one of his problem players (Lew Ayres).

Dame. In 1932 MGM picked up one of his college football novels called *Huddle* and, apparently for the sake of variety moved the locale of the story from South Bend to the Yale campus at New Haven, another hotbed of the gridiron sport during this time. In spite of this transition, Wallace's basic story line remains the same: a headstrong football player (Ramón Navarro) learns a great deal about himself and life through his involvement in the game. As one of the longest films of the gridiron genre, *Huddle* takes its hero, in ever so anticlimactic fashion, from his freshman to his senior year amid a variety of soap-opera situations before he undergoes the necessary character transformations in the last reel and wins not only the big game but the girl (Madge Evans) and a college degree as well.[16]

Actually, in 1931 Paramount had been the first studio to film a Wallace story when it purchased his novel *Stadium* as the source for another of its catchy one-word titles, a picture called *Touchdown,* which added a unique twist to the usual football tale. Richard Arlen, playing a former all-American football star who becomes a major college coach, has something in common with all coaches in that he hates to lose. Where he differs from most coaches is in his abusive treatment of players because of his obsessive drive to win at all costs. After ordering an injured player back into a game, a decision which sends the player to the hospital, Arlen loses the respect of not only his players but also his associates and girl friend (Peggy Shannon). To make a hero out of a heel, the movie's climax finds Arlen faced with a familiar dilemma: whether or not to send an injured player back into the game and risk the chance of a fatal injury. His decision to keep the player on the sidelines naturally redeems the respect of his players and his girl, but he winds up losing the game—one of the few times that the moral lesson of a football film allows this to happen. Once again, the familiar face of Jack Oakie shows up for comic relief while an assortment of well-known football personalities puts in an appearance, including Jim Thorpe, University of Southern California coach Howard Jones, and players Roy "Wrong-Way" Riegels and Herman Brix, who would soon become known as the movie star Bruce Bennett.[17]

Richard Arlen (1898–1976), destined to become one of the most popular B movie heroes of the 1940s, was among the most convincing acting talents of the college-life tradition during the 1930s. He showed up once again in Universal's *The All-American* (1932), a film praised primarily for its departure from formula "by taking the game of football apart instead of making it 100% heroism. . . ."[18] In fact, this picture starts where most football films end—with hero Arlen's last starring performance for his school. The dramatic intent here is to contrast Arlen's gridiron triumphs with his ensuing downhill slide, the result of his wild life-style after he quits school. He wakes up in time to discover that his kid brother, also an all-American type, may be about to follow in his older brother's footsteps. Arlen is then prompted to play in an all-star game comprised of famous past players who compete against a team of current players including his brother. Arlen's plan, of course, is to show the kid a thing or two about how to play the game of football as well as teach him a lesson, which he does. The movie ends on a note of reconciliation, with both brothers apparently finding themselves. In this serious exploration of the college football player as a human being with problems that extend beyond those of the playing field, we witness a psychological approach to the athletic experience that would set a trend for many films to follow. To bring in some comedy relief, though, *The All-American* had Andy Devine. Universal's answer to Jack Oakie, Devine was an easygoing, likable sort who was to go on as Richard Arlen's dumb but well-meaning sidekick in a number of B movies in the 1940s.[19]

Perhaps as a reaction to the rather worn image of the clean-cut college man, the Arlen football dramas apparently started a move toward the antihero cast as a college football player. *Saturday's Millions* (Universal, 1933), a picture whose title referred to game attendance but could just as well have meant the money generated by these events, was another story in the same antiheroic mold. Robert Young is a football star with a less than enthusiastic attitude toward both the game and life, but a girl (Leila Hyams) helps transform his outlook and personality, with the ironic outcome that even though he loses the big game by fumbling on the goal line, he does manage to win the girl. (Referring to this latest trend in football stories, a reviewer of this film lamented that it would be refreshing "to see an old-fashioned hero who makes the 90-yard winning sprint in the last half minute of the very last period."[20] Obviously, it didn't take the movie critics very long to tire of any new development in the football drama.) Lending support to Young in *Saturday's Millions* is real-life football star Johnny Mack Brown as his running mate and Andy Devine continuing his string of collegiate appearances in another comedy role. But the prize for inspired comic acting in this film would have to go to Grant Mitchell and Richard Tucker as a couple of old grads who haven't seen each other in forty years and nostalgically retrogress to the behavior of their younger days.

MGM also subscribed to the popular antihero football star of this era with *The Band Plays On* (1934), which despite its title was not a musical. The picture tells the story of four street-wise youths—of whom Robert Young is the leader—who steal a car for fun and when they are caught find themselves assigned to the custody of a football coach who runs a summer playground. The coach (Preston Foster) takes a deep interest in them and trains the boys to perform as a super backfield, which becomes good enough in fact to star at a big West Coast school. After some disruptive problems that alienate the boys from the other members of their team, they come around in time to rejoin the squad and play together in the big game. Something about this film's special concern with the rehabilitation of street kids looked ahead to the popular Dead End Kid series of the late 1930s—a concern which implies that probably the main influence on the trend toward negative characterization in football dramas at that time was the exceptional popularity of gangster movies. If social conflict was the major dramatic ingredient of most college-life movie plots, then it was easy enough to develop the criminal type of character for a role in this kind of movie.

For example, the implausible plot of RKO's *Gridiron Flash* (1934) had Eddie Quillan in the part of a paroled convict playing for a big-time college team. Alumnus Grant Mitchell discovers the talented Quillan playing on a prison team and somehow manages to wrangle a pardon for him to play for Mitchell's alma mater. Naturally, his new-

In keeping with the antihero trend of the 1930s, Eddie Quillan plays an ex-convict turned football star in *Gridiron Flash* (RKO, 1934). Alumnus supporter Grant Mitchell looks on.

found freedom presents Quillan with some problems, particularly when he is tempted to fall back into his old ways by stealing some jewelry. However, he realizes for the first time that his collegiate experiences have made a new man of him, and the ex-convict turns from his errant ways to win the big game for his school. From a larger perspective, Eddie Quillan's role in *Gridiron Flash* was really just another variation on the theme of the underdog who through revitalization of the self gets the upper hand in the end. This remained a very popular theme in the Depression years simply because it commanded a great deal of audience identification.

Actually, the cliché ending of the football drama had not died out as the *Variety* reviewer had opined, for in the same year (1933) as *Saturday's Millions* Warner Brothers' *College Coach* appeared. This picture had one of the most sensational big-game endings of all serious football movies. With ten minutes to go, the score is 20–0 against Dick Powell's team, but he somehow manages to score three touchdowns and as many extra points to win at the gun, 21–20. In spite of the sensational ending, this movie was noteworthy for the performance of Pat O'Brien, whose role as a dedicated coach helped him warm up for his memorable casting in 1940 as Knute Rockne in *Knute Rockne—All American* (Warner Bros.). O'Brien's firm, decisive manner tempered by his basically human reaction to his players and their problems made him a natural for the accepted public image of the college football coach, and as such he is the dominant presence in *College Coach*. Dick Powell is refreshing in his attempt to break the

In *College Coach* (Warner Bros., 1933), Pat O'Brien was warming up for his future role as Knute Rockne.

mold of the stereotypical football player. He sings a song and surprisingly seems to be more interested in getting an education than he does a girl, but somehow Powell's innocent good looks belie his role as a rugged all-star football player.

In 1936, the conventional hero of football drama cropped up again in RKO's *The Big Game,* another Francis Wallace story adapted to the screen by Irwin Shaw. It would seem strange that no one had ever thought of college football's big event for a movie title until this time, but perhaps the reason was because such a title promised too much. At any rate, *The Big Game* had a tough time living up to its name, and turned out to be just another going over of the same tired situations in which the film's unlikely hero (Philip Huston) is involved: his kidnapping and entrapment by big-time gamblers in the exploitation of the game, his relationship with players recruited from the coal mining fields (Andy Devine, in particular), and his appearance with real-life all-Americans who have supporting roles. It must have been a bit too much for viewers to take when they discovered that these recognized super athletes couldn't win without their kidnapped "star." Nevertheless, one critic assessed the collegiate football drama as being still very much alive when he rated *The Big Game* as "both timely and okay entertainment for the not so particular gridiron addict."[21]

Tom Brown, whose perennially youthful looks were undoubtedly the main reason for his appearance in a number of college-life movies during this era, had the lead roles in two other football dramas that depended on the genre's standard plot ingredients. *Rose Bowl* (Paramount, 1936) was a typical Hollywood ploy to incorporate in its title a well-known event to help sell the picture. Even though the script was once again from the fertile pen of Francis Wallace, it was one of his poorest efforts, and *Rose Bowl* turned out to be just another gridiron caper.[22] In Universal's *Swing That Cheer* (1938)—which, incidentally, was not a musical—Tom Brown is a football hero who gets a case of the athlete's social disease—the swelled head. After coming to the realization that it is the blocking and interference of his teammates that have helped make him a star, Brown becomes generous enough to allow his blocking back to score the winning points in the big game, and everything closes happily, as one reviewer put it, with "the cute co-ed running on the field for the fadeout clinch at the whistle."[23] It may appear that by the late 1930s and the advent of a film like *Swing That Cheer,* the collegiate football drama had run its course, but as we shall see, this kind of movie resurfaced from time to time in the 1940s and 1950s. As the most collegiately representative of competitive sports, football had made its mark on the social consciousness of the American moviegoing public.

A persistent technical problem of the football films of the 1930s was finding a way to overcome the obvious visual difference between filming close-ups and long shots of football plays. In most cases from the 1920s on, studios relied on newsreel footage for game color and crowd atmosphere, intersplicing these shots with their regular story line coverage of the actual performers. The overall effect, except in some isolated instances, was incongruous, and reviewers of the period were quick to point out the problem. Typically, a review of *The Band Plays On,* in noting the newsreel footage that had been spliced in, observed that "there is too much of it but not much that's very exciting."[24] Very seldom did a studio receive the praise that MGM did for its 1929 production of *So This Is College* when a critic wrote that this studio

> was the first to take its cue from the newsreel grid stuff to give the hero a number which matched the ground gainer in the news shots. Also, if memory serves, this plant was the first to follow the genuine play in that the closeup matter was made to coincide with the team information shown in the news clip. That is, when the press stand view shows somebody starting around end, or fading back to heave a pass, the prop closeup action picks up the same play half way through to magnify its completion.[25]

But nearly a decade later some moviemakers had still not profited by the example of others, and a reviewer of Warner Brothers' *Over the Goal* could remark in 1937 that even though "the long shots of actual college games are convincing and exciting. . . . the action closeups are pretty dreadful."[26] Not until *Saturday's Hero* in 1951 would this bothersome aspect of the football drama achieve the technical perfection that would convince viewers they were watching the real thing.

However, most moviegoers of the 1930s were prone to overlook any visual imperfections for the attraction of an appealing story or setting that could supersede any technical weakness. College itself was remote enough from the average moviegoer's personal life as to appear somewhat romantic and exotic, and this condition was no doubt what motivated many directors and scriptwriters to come up with their peculiar admixture of athletics, social life, and the collegiate experience. Due to the era's pervasive hunger for fantasy identification and novel forms of entertainment, movie audiences of the 1930s revealed a naïveté that generally saw nothing wrong with what Hollywood had to offer and the way in which it was offered. Whether expressed musically, comically, or melodramatically, the college-life movie had wide appeal, particularly for the nation's youth at whom it appeared to be mainly directed. In dramatizing stories whose complications were readily resolved, these films treated human relationships in an oversimplified and idealized fashion, ignoring in most cases any reference to the problems of the outside world or the routine pursuits that were so much a part of a student's real-life existence. As a result, the college-oriented movie must have inspired many a high-school youth to be a part of the glamorous life-style they saw on the screen. At the same time, the fantasy world these films projected must have titillated older people who had never gone to college into thinking that they had greatly missed out by not having attended. By the middle of the 1930s, the familiar stage imagery and plot conventions of the collegiate film variations had been established, and popular audiences were visually conditioned to expect certain patterns in Hollywood's special interpretation of college life. Hollywood, of course, was presenting what it thought moviegoers wanted to see. In time, this special view of reality would contribute to our present-day nostalgic fascination with the 1930s and the myriad movies of the period. For further illustration, we need now to look at other variations of the college-life movie during the 1930s that also contributed to this fascination.

In the realm of pure comedy, the name of Joe E. Brown (1891–1973) was popular in the movies of the 1930s. Brown's personal trademark was an exceptionally wide mouth, which he used to comic advantage in his brand of slapstick antics. An ex-athlete and circus-vaudeville performer, he came through in a number of roles that called for fancy acrobatics and bone-shattering falls in the Buster Keaton tradition. In *Maybe It's Love* (Warner Brothers, 1930), Joe dominates the action as "Speed" Hanson, an effervesent collegiate type whose comic performance counteracts the role of Joan Bennett, the college president's daughter. As the standard college widow, Joan is naturally bent on attracting superior football players to her school. As though to support her efforts, this film actually signed up an entire real-life all-American football team, but a great deal more than this was needed to save this film from mediocrity.

In 1939, Joe E. Brown costarred with Martha Raye, his equally wide-mouthed feminine counterpart, in an unusual collegiate film called *$1,000 a Touchdown* (Paramount). The plot of this movie, particularly in its treatment of college football, is among the most absurd ever written by a Hollywood scriptwriter. As another variation of the hackneyed college inheritance theme, the story has Miss Raye inheriting a campus where no students show up. She then decides that what the school needs is a football team.[27] Because the team doesn't have a regular schedule drawn up yet, Miss Raye proposes that the college play a professional team, an on-the-field agreement being that the pro team be given $1,000 for every touchdown that it allows her school to score. The situation is so contrived, of course, that the question of team honor hardly enters the picture since a large sum of money can be won simply by falling down. It is Brown himself, in one of his weakest roles, who settles everything when he is "allowed" to win the game in the final minutes. This movie is interesting, though, if only because it exemplifies the ridiculous lengths that scriptwriters felt compelled to go to to come up with novel variations in an overworked mode.

Brown's best college-life picture was *The Gladiator* (Columbia, 1938), a loose adaptation of Philip Wylie's novel of the same name and something of a throwback to Harold Lloyd's search for social identity in *The Freshman*. In 1931, Brown had appeared in a remake of 1927's *The Poor Nut* called *Local Boy Makes Good* (First National) in which his role as a misfit is reminiscent of Lloyd's and Keaton's collegiate film efforts and prophetic of certain scenes in *The Gladiator*.[28] In developing Wylie's "superman" premise in the latter film, Brown plays an ineffectual fellow named Hugo Kipp, who wins a sizable sum of money and decides to return to college—after twelve years—and enter his sophomore year. Older and more set in his ways, Hugo is naturally subject to considerable razzing from his fellow students—a predicament that sets the stage for his dramatic transformation into an individual they can no longer afford to abuse. When Hugo meets up with a professor right out of the crackpot mold, the prof injects him with a serum that changes Hugo into a person with superhuman powers. Needless to say, Hugo's social life takes a different tack right away. He becomes a star on the football team and, in one of the film's highlights, manages to throw Man Mountain Dean, a popular professional wrestler of the day. Naturally, the students begin to see Hugo in a different light, and in typical collegiate film fashion, he wins over his girl (June Travis) in the end.

The Gladiator is significantly different from its prototypes in that while both Lloyd and Keaton are allowed to find themselves psychologically through the discovery of inner resources they never knew they possessed, Brown has to resort to a scientific formula to become a social entity—an artificial method that tells us something about Hollywood's changing attitude toward social identity and the role of personal development in the late 1930s. In one other major respect, though, *The Gladiator* was very much like its predecessors, and that was in its depiction of hero Brown's relationship with his woman.

In most college-life movies, women play a variety of roles that dramatize the disparity between the high expectations generated by the hero's personal ideals or goals and the realities of his social setting. These character types may range in function from that of a Jobyna Ralston in *The Freshman* or a June Travis in *The Gladiator* (whose dramatic intent is to inspire their men to overcome their ineptitude), to that of a campus flirt like Clara Bow in *The Wild Party* or a college widow like Joan Bennett in *Maybe It's Love* (whose major purpose, it seems, is to stir up a series of problems for the protagonist or lead characters). Whether bent on goodwill or deception, though, the leading lady of a college-life movie is always a highly attractive

June Travis helped inspire Joe E. Brown's gridiron heroics in his best collegiate film, *The Gladiator* **(Columbia, 1938).**

girl whose physical bearing attests to Hollywood's idealized concept of what the public thinks the American college girl should look like. From the contrasting types played by Delores Costello and Clara Bow in the 1920s through Betty Grable and June Travis in the 1930s to Ali McGraw and Lindsay Wagner in the 1970s, we have witnessed this interpretation. From the Hollywood point of view, we might wonder if a less than attractive girl ever went to college.

In many of these films, it is the campus flirt who, because she relishes going to great lengths to make things miserable for the males in her life, carries more dramatic impact than that of any other female role. For example, in *College Lovers* (First National, 1930), co-ed Marion Nixon openly delights in alienating her school's star football players (Guinn Williams and Russell Hopton) by her affections when all the while she is really after the team's student manager (Jack Whiting). By the time the two naïve players learn the truth, they are into the second half of the big game with an opportunity to score the winning touchdown. But after having been romantic rivals for so long, they suddenly become overly polite, each player offering the other the chance to score, thus ironically frittering away the final

During the 1930s the popular conception of the college girl was expressed in roles like those of cheerleaders Priscilla and Rosemary Lane in *Varsity Show* (Warner Bros., 1937).

minute until the game ends in a tie. In the college-life movie, the influence of women was so pervasive that it extended even to the all-male athletic scene.[29]

On a much more sophisticated level, the social role of women was an important element in dramatizing the farcical relationship of the sexes. Inspired by a Phillip Barry play, *Spring Madness* (MGM, 1938) was a collegiate version of the screwball comedy that was so popular during this era. The world of woman, as it was interpreted in this Hollywood genre, was one of romantic entanglements and sexual innuendo in which the woman always held the upper hand. By over-looking the sports angle of the typical collegiate movie, *Spring Madness* was not only a refreshing respite, it demonstrated that the collegiate scene could generate a more mature brand of entertainment than it had in the past. Lew Ayres is a Harvard man who romances a Radcliffe girl, played by Maureen O'Sullivan, but their relationship is complicated by Ayres's roommate (Burgess Meredith), an avowed misogynist looking forward to traveling abroad with Ayres upon their graduation. Perhaps due to the time's more innocent portrayal of male friendships, the underlying implications of this relationship are ignored for the more conventional situation of a fraternal bond be-tween Ayres and Burgess, and after a series of wacky entanglements, everything reaches a happy conclusion in the usual screwball man-ner. In spite of its talented cast, the film version of *Spring Madness* comes across as average entertainment, but it does represent one of the more original attempts to portray the social side of the collegiate experience in a more down-to-earth manner.

In the same comedic vein that would peak in 1942 with *The Male Animal* was *Vivacious Lady* (RKO, 1938), which costarred Ginger Rogers and James Stewart. Enhanced by the directing skills of the talented George Stevens, this film has Stewart playing a college pro-fessor who falls in love with nightclub singer Rogers, whom he mar-ries after a whirlwind courtship. Stevens's approach is to reveal how the marriage of individuals from different social strata can contribute to prejudicial attitudes that have been fostered by the canons of re-spectability. As the son of the college president, who is admirably played by a college-film stalwart Charles Coburn, Stewart is faced with the difficult task of breaking the news of his marriage to his domineering and tradition-bound parents. Both their immediate reac-tion to his announcement and the manner in which a compromise is ultimately worked out make for a highly entertaining view of the patrician attitude toward the democratic process.

With only a very few exceptions, such as Donald Sutherland's unconventional role in *Animal House* (1978), the social function of the college professor in the movies has been governed by a special code of behavior expectations throughout the past sixty years. Like

College prof James Stewart and companion share a microscope as an envious Ginger Rogers looks on in *Vivacious Lady* (RKO, 1938).

the minister, the academician on his pedestal of moral uprightness has always been fair game for both literature and the movies. A German film, *The Blue Angel,* set the precedent for this kind of thing in 1930 with the story of a professor (Emil Jannings) who falls in love with a tawdry nightclub singer (Marlene Dietrich), but in the America of 1938, a college professor marrying a nightclub entertainer was indeed a unique gesture, even in the guise of comedy.[30] Ironically, *Vivacious Lady,* like most comedies that deal with the complexities of social relationships, bordered on the serious. It was an attitude that would shortly become more common in the college-life movie.

During the 1930s the college-life movie was a naturally popular vehicle for introducing new faces and fresh personalities to the Hollywood scene, particularly the type known popularly as the "starlet": Loretta Young, Betty Grable, and Susan Hayward, for example. One of these hopefuls was a teenager who would soon become legendary—Lana Turner. In 1939, while not yet twenty, Miss Turner was cast in two MGM films with collegiate themes, *Dancing Co-ed* and *These Glamour Girls.* In the first film she had a rather innocuous part opposite her first husband-to-be—bandleader Artie Shaw. Such co-ed roles were especially attractive for a promising young beauty to ingratiate herself with movie audiences, even though they rarely called for any more talent than just to look pretty. However, in *These Glamour Girls,* Miss Turner won a degree of critical acclaim in her first major role. She played a social rebel whose uncooperative manner helped undermine what was supposed to have been a swanky college weekend of social activity. Obviously, the basic theme of the college-life movie was still alive in 1939. The excellent cast, which included Lew Ayres as well as performers in the collegiate tradition like Tom Brown, Richard Carlson, Ann Rutherford, Anita Louise, and Marsha Hunt, was involved in a screwball plot centered around the interrelationship of six collegiate romances—a rather ambitious dramatic undertaking for the college-life genre at this time.

That other attractive blonde, Betty Grable, was still being typecast as "Betty Co-ed" during the late 1930s, appearing in several collegiate films other than musicals. In one of the more misleadingly titled movies, *Million Dollar Legs* (Paramount, 1939), she at last received top billing over the other stars—Donald O'Connor, Jackie Coogan,

In *Dancing Co-ed* (MGM, 1939), Lana Turner, at nineteen, confronts a professor— Monty Woolley, who in real life had been a member of the Yale faculty before turning to acting. Richard Carlson (left) and Benny Baker look on.

Peter Lind Hayes, and Buster Crabbe—but again she received no promising reviews for yet another college coquette performance.[31] This story is about a down-and-out college rowing crew that needs a new rowing shell in order to compete effectively. A horse-race tip results in a long shot win for crew member Hayes, the acquisition of the new shell, and, of course, the obligatory win over their big rivals. Considering the highly publicized shapely figure for which Miss Grable eventually became famous, we could easily be misled as to whether the title of this film refers to her, the winning race horse, or the crew members. At any rate, even with Betty Grable in a starring role in a proven popular genre, this picture did not make much of a splash, one reason being that *Million Dollar Legs* was one of Paramount's periodic vehicles for testing its younger contract players. Among those assigned to this film was the promising but now forgotten John Hartley, Betty's love interest. Hartley's stock character here is the campus rich boy who tries to make it on his own without his father's help. This was a situation that was central to the plot of another of Betty Grable's melodramatic films of college life— *Campus Confessions* (Paramount, 1938).

By the time of Betty's lead role in this film, sports fans were becoming basketball conscious, mainly because of the revolutionary play of all-American Hank Luisetti of Stanford University. Following the tradition of signing up popular athletes for movie roles, Paramount scooped the other lots by contracting the talented Luisetti for *Campus Confessions*. The first player to open up the game of basketball with a free-wheeling, individualistic style of play, Luisetti was spotlighted not only to show off his playing ability but to function as an inspiration to William Henry, a misunderstood rich-boy type who is compelled to seek campus popularity in a manner similar to that of Speedy Lamb in *The Freshman*. To dramatize its variation on the rich-boy theme, *Campus Confessions* casts Betty Grable as a coquettish co-ed who gives Henry a socially rough time until he finally proves himself a winner in basketball—which also opens the way for him to shake off the dominance of his wealthy but antiathletic father. During the Depression years, the rich father image was apparently one that audiences loved to hate, and it frequently crops up, particularly in numerous college-life movies of the period. The heroic figure of a well-to-do young man disavowing any need for financial assistance and setting out on his own must have struck a responsive chord in the average moviegoer during the 1930s. Once again, Miss Grable, in her usual college girl role, was passed over by the critics, who remained noncommittal concerning her acting ability. Even though she would never be praised for quality acting, Betty Grable was among the most familiar figures of the college-life movie tradition, and would develop into one of the most popular stars of the

1940s in the technicolor Fox musical fantasies. Many of her contemporaries did not fare so well.

Some films valiantly tried to break away from the clichés of the typical collegiate movie of the 1930s. One that could have been turned into an effective piece of satire, had it been handled properly, was MGM's *We Went to College* (1936). The Homecoming weekend, which is the inspiration for this movie's plot, has actually never been explored as fully as it could have been with respect to the dramatic intent of revealing what happened to the old grads in the years since they left school. There have been a few outstanding attempts at dramatizing postcollege experiences, most notably *The Group* (1966) and *The Graduate* (1967), but these films tend to ignore the direct social involvement of the campus environment that the college-life film genre demands. Unfortunately, in *We Went to College* the familiar stereotyped roles prevent this picture from creating a reasonably realistic interpretation of one of the most fascinating activities of the American social scene—the alumni reunion. Charles Butterworth plays the familiar drunk alumnus who even goes so far as to run out on the field during the homecoming game to singlehandedly halt the progress of a player on the opposing team. The professorial type comes in for his usual share of derision in Hugh Herbert's performance as an absent-minded academic. However, Una Merkel, a seasoned character actress, turns in the best performance of the movie as the professor's continually complaining wife. Then there's Walter Abel taking on the part of a successful businessman whose real reason for attending the reunion is not to renew old ties but to further his business contacts. Overall, though, *We Went to College* misses out on a golden opportunity to capture one of the college experience's most socially significant events, when alumni create a setting in which they try to recapture the golden moments of a vanished youth.

Paramount decided that using the murder mystery formula at a campus locale might enliven the standard collegiate scene that audiences had become accustomed to. So, in *College Scandal* (1935), the familiar device of students putting on a big show became the background for murder. After two students are done away with, concerned fellow students do some detective work to nab the murderer before he can strike again. Making the most of a cast that included the acting talents of Arline Judge, Kent Taylor, Wendy Barrie, and William Frawley, this film would get a bigger play in 1942 when it was remade by Paramount as a musical called *Sweater Girl,* starring Eddie Bracken (see chapter 3).

The popularity of series like MGM's *Thin Man* probably led Paramount to turn out its own version of the comedy mystery called *Murder Goes to College* (1937). Important reasons for the comic success of this film are the acting and repartée of Roscoe Karns as a

Murder on the campus inspired the plot of *College Scandal* (Paramount, 1935), an entertaining film with a lackluster cast. Here, Wendy Barrie (in checked outfit) concerns herself with what looks like another corpse.

bottle-nipping reporter and Lynne Overman as a wisecracking detective, both bent on solving the murder of a college professor. A script that waits until the last possible moment to reveal the killer's identity greatly enhances this movie's dramatic impact and places it squarely in the tradition of the Hollywood "whodunit" movie. Romantic interest is supplied by Marsha Hunt, and once again Larry "Buster" Crabbe appears in a collegiate movie, this time in the role of a murder suspect.[32]

Even as they attempted to come up with novel plots, these pictures continued to portray college-related characters as stereotypes and lackeys to the system. Perhaps they tried, in their way, to be realistic about the collegiate experience, but it is obvious that Hollywood continued to see the college campus as a remote, ivory-tower setting—a kind of fantasized background that is isolated from the mainstream of society. Ironically, this very remoteness is what attracted both moviemakers and moviegoers, for it was a setting that fostered the illusion of almost unlimited dramatic possibilities.

Accordingly, some collegiate movies produced during the 1930s attempted to counteract the general escapist mood in order to express a serious theme. In 1931, Paramount experimented with the sensitive area of premarital sex in *Confessions of a Co-ed,* when Sylvia Sidney carries her necking parties a little too far and winds up pregnant. Much of the soap-opera plot concentrates on what happens when Miss Sidney out of social necessity marries a boy friend who is not the father of her child. What we have here, of course, is really another version of the old triangular relationship. After the real father returns from abroad, certain obligatory revelations appear to square everything for the acting principals—but not for the film critics. Mordaunt Hall, writing in *The New York Times,* called it "a most trivial and implausible story," nothing more than "a Hollywood conception of an educational institution, where as usual, the students devote their whole time to discussing affairs of the heart, never for an instant revealing any inclination of work."[33] Mr. Hall was, of course, merely describing the general Hollywood interpretation of the college campus in the 1930s as a place where social activity always had priority over any kind of academic endeavor.

In RKO's *Age of Consent* (1932), the problem of a young couple (Dorothy Wilson and Richard Cromwell) deciding whether or not to quit school and get married is sensitively explored. Also, the image of the college professor as a wise old sage is presented for the first time in a film that was well received by the critics. Actually, the professorial role, expertly played by John Halliday, is a bridge between the generation gap, and as one reviewer expressed it, this film's chief virtue is to dramatize the wild side of campus behavior and "filter its meaning through the complacent eyes of the old professor . . . who sees in the whoopee of the youngsters only youthful spirits, inevitable and natural. 'We called it sparking when I was young,' he comments. 'Now they call it necking.' "[34] This remark in itself tells us how distant the year 1932 is from the 1980s.

RKO also turned out another interesting collegiate film in *Finishing School* (1934), which concentrated on the conflict between social expression and institutional restrictions. Frances Dee and Ginger Rogers are students in a well-to-do but straitlaced and strict girls' school where their personal lives run afoul of the rules and regulations. In fact, the credits to this movie go so far as to announce that the movie's principal villain is the school itself, a place where the rules are set to keep the students from tarnishing its impeccable image. The storyline has Miss Dee falling in love with a young man who is considered to be beneath the school's social level. In spite of the enforced rules and regulations, love naturally wins out in the end as if to make the point that human relationships cannot be regulated. Ginger Rogers has one of the film's more refreshing roles as an unconventional student who thrives on seeing how many of the school's rules she can break and get away with. "You can do anything you

like," she surmises, "as long as you don't get caught." In the entire
college-life tradition, her comment is the one most representative of
the student's relationship with the system of higher education.

Sorority House (1939) continued RKO's serious approach to the
social concerns of the collegiate experience, reflecting a trend that
would carry over into the 1940s. Anne Shirley is the central figure of
this film, which examines the effects of sorority life on a first-year
student from a background of ordinary means.[35] Encouraged to become a member of the most snobbish sorority on campus, Miss Shirley is compelled by group pressure to ignore her self-sacrificing
father, a grocer who has used his life savings to send her to college.[36]
Finally realizing her self-centered attitude, she turns down the sorority's bid for membership and organizes her own "social club" with
several of her antisorority classmates. Although her boy friend James
Ellison is the campus football hero, this film is unique in avoiding
athletics to concentrate on sorority politics. The snobbish and elitist
sorority leaders are the real villains of *Sorority House,* which revealed an increasing social consciousness at that time concerning the
real worth of the sorority-fraternity system.[37]

**The prototype for films about sorority life may have been *Finishing School* (RKO, 1934)
with its story about the strict rules of a girls' school. Sarah Haden is the instructor, and
to her immediate left are students Frances Dee and Ginger Rogers.**

Another popular type of collegiate movie, and one with a wide-spread inspirational impact during the 1930s, was that dealing with student life in the service academies. Remembering that the first World War was only a decade away and that rumors of another war were building helps us understand the popular feeling toward the military at this time. Because of the disciplinary demands of military life, in marked contrast to the more individualistic and relaxed life-style of the civilian student, the academy administration and its hierarchy play more of a dramatic role in these films. In many cases, they represent the protagonist's dramatic adversary to be reckoned with and overcome. During the years between the two world wars, when the American society still retained something of an innocent outlook on political behavior, movies with a military academy back-ground reflected the same basic concerns as did their civilian school counterparts, the main difference being that the actors of a service school film wore uniforms.

The most common plot formula in these films appears to be the triangular relationship in which two rivals vie for the same girl (or fellow). This convention can be traced to an early silent Biograph film *Classmates* (1914), also noteworthy as one of Lionel Barrymore's first screen appearances. In this picture, two West Point appointees, one wealthy but self-centered (Marshall Neilan), the other poor but honest (Henry Walthall), pursue the same girl (Blanche Sweet). After a fight, both cadets are expelled, but later, in a foreign country, Neilan is rescued from a perilous situation by his former classmate. Walthall is then exonerated and winds up with the girl. *Classmates* was remade in 1924 by Inspiration Pictures, and starred Richard Barthelmess and Madge Evans. Largely due to its realism, which resulted from its scenes shot on location, this film received good reviews and played to big crowds. In fact, one reviewer was so taken by it that he felt the "West Point angle alone" was enough to have made a success out of any film.[38] At this point in the development of the Hollywood movie, naïve critics of course knew very little about how rapidly public taste could change.

At any rate, the reviewer of *The Midshipman* (MGM), the Naval Academy's equal-time movie in 1925, observed that this film, as well as *Classmates,* had missed out by not including the annual Army-Navy football game in the climactic build-up. Because of the natural rivalry between these two branches of the military, the general feeling must have been that these traditional adversaries should meet in a showdown confrontation. Disappointed by this oversight, the *Variety* critic informed his readers that "The Cadets and Middies are surefire subjects, always have been and always will be."[39] Typically, he pos-sessed the acutely limited vision of his peers, because by the 1930s reviewers would be complaining of an overdose of the kind of fare that climaxes predictably with the big game, whether civilian or military.

In its day, though, *The Midshipman,* with Ramón Navarro in the starring role, was a popular favorite. Its story was nothing more than a routine affair, but its attention to realistic detail in the scenes shot on location caught the public imagination. With the permission of the Navy Department, cameras recorded two dress parades, an actual mess-hall scene, the June Ball, and the graduating exercises with the real-life Secretary of the Navy giving out diplomas. Navarro was even allowed to get in line with the rest of the candidates to receive an unofficial degree. The military school film was one of the pioneer movie genres to rely on the actual setting of its story to project realism on the screen, and audiences loved what they saw.

When two films about West Point appeared in 1927, it began to look as though the cadets were taking the show away from the middies of Annapolis.[40] William Haines costarred with Joan Crawford in *West Point* (MGM), and William Boyd, who had had a part in *The Midshipman,* followed up with the lead role in *Dress Parade* (Pathé). In the former film, Haines plays the stock know-it-all type who has his personality revamped by Miss Crawford in time to become a dedicated football player and score the winning touchdown against Navy. The Boyd vehicle suffers from a weak story line and a surfeit of sentiment. Often in the 1920s—perhaps due to the lingering influence of World War I—directors of military school movies felt compelled to emphasize the patriotic angle by focusing on the lead player's dedication to the academy. Even so, it was a posture that did not become dated until the 1950s when the controversial Korean conflict generated a more cynical attitude toward the military, both in the movies and in real life. In *Dress Parade,* the moviemakers' quest for realism to underscore their patriotic premise is again evident in the number of scenes that were shot on location. The primary historical interest of this film for later Boyd fans is that it gives them a view of the perennially silver-maned actor some years before he became permanently typed as the popular cowboy hero Hopalong Cassidy.

More than any other film director, John Ford revealed a sensitivity to the implications of the intense rivalry between military academies when he directed a 1929 film called *Salute* (Fox). His approach was also original in that he attempted to capture both academies' points of view in the same film.[41] George O'Brien as a West Pointer and William Janney as a midshipman play brothers who eventually meet as adversaries on the gridiron. With each brother scoring a touchdown, the game fittingly ends in a tie, as though to symbolize the important but equal contribution of each institution to American military strength. In spite of its rather predictable ending, the film's romantic intrigue and comedy interludes are of high enough quality to make it entertaining fare. Featuring two Southern California teammates named Ward Bond and John Wayne (Marion Morrison), *Salute* favorably impressed one reviewer to the extent that he rated it "with *Brown of Harvard* as the best picture of its kind to date."[42]

Just as the Hollywood musical had idealized the civilian version of college, so a 1934 musical called *Flirtation Walk* (Warner Brothers) helped glamorize student life in a service academy more than any other movie had up to that time. The West Point setting is offset by Dick Powell's singing, Ruby Keeler's acting (surprisingly, she does not dance in this film), and Pat O'Brien's appealing and dependable Irish manner. Typically, the story line derives from the conflicts of rank and problems in discipline attendant to military life—a highly rigid system that in enticing the individual to challenge it is capable of creating comic as well as dramatic impact.

The very next year, Warner Brothers gave the Navy its fair share of musical recognition with *Shipmates Forever,* yet another picture highlighting the team of Powell and Keeler. This one depicts Powell as a rebel against family tradition in that he'd rather be a singer than a sailor. He goes on to Annapolis anyway, and after rescuing a classmate from a perilous predicament, finds himself becoming a dedicated Navy man in the finest family tradition. As in most musicals, the song-and-dance numbers keep intruding on the story's natural development, but a notable feature of *Shipmates Forever* was its outstanding score by the talented team of Harry Warren and Al Dubin.

In keeping pace with the other studios that were turning out military school features during this time, MGM, which had effected a stamp of quality peculiarly its own, came up with one of the most popular service academy films of the 1930s in *Navy Blue and Gold* (1937). MGM films always emphasized strong characterization within a unique kind of setting, and by approaching and developing its subject matter from a more psychological perspective than that of the usual military school movie, *Navy Blue and Gold* enjoyed healthy box-office returns and also contributed a great deal to perpetuating the Naval Academy mystique among the general public. James Stewart, Robert Young, and Tom Brown—all veterans of the collegiate movie—play distinctively different personalities whose involvement with each other goes beyond traditional academy concerns and the usual dormitory pranks to the football field, where they discover a common identity in playing for the Navy varsity. A long-running personal feud between Stewart and Young, which forms the basis for the film's dramatic conflict, is finally resolved in the big game with Army. With the score tied, Young, led by Stewart's blocking, breaks loose from the defense, but in the most gentlemanly of acts ever included in a big-game finale, he hands the ball back to

Stewart to score the winning touchdown. Such generosity may have greatly appealed to movie audiences, but this situation mainly served to show how Hollywood was still straining for new variations on an old theme. In the service academy movies that followed, screenwriters came up with a myriad of ways to resolve the chronic personal animosities and psychological conflicts that plagued the inmates of the Hollywood military school.

By the middle of the 1930s the Army-Navy rivalry had obviously caught the public's fancy, and this plot situation continued to crop up over the remainder of the decade and on into the 1940s in a number of minor movie entries.[43] But it was 1938—a golden year for all collegiate-type movies—that came up with two of the most unusual approaches to dramatizing military-school life: *Duke of West Point* (United Artists) and *Brother Rat* (Warner Brothers). The former film was actually a reverse twist on MGM's *A Yank at Oxford* (1938), which starred Robert Taylor as a brash young American student trying to adjust to the British traditions of Oxford University.[44] *Duke,* on the other hand, cast Louis Hayward as a Cambridge rugby star who is

Standing tall before their superiors are James Stewart, Tom Brown, and Robert Young in *Navy Blue and Gold* (MGM, 1937), one of the most popular military school films of the 1930s.

sent to the U.S. Military Academy by his father in order to enhance
the honor of a military-oriented family. While at West Point, Hayward becomes involved with a rival for the affections of Joan Fon-
taine, who was just beginning to make a name for herself in starring
roles at this time. Instead of the obligatory football game to test the
mettle of the hero, *Duke of West Point* presented audiences with the
then relatively uncommon sport of ice hockey. This switch no doubt
derived from the feeling that ice hockey complemented Hayward's
designation and reputation as an accomplished rugby player—a game
completely unknown to most Americans. Even so, the most
significant contribution of this film to the collegiate tradition was its
depiction of Louis Hayward as an appealing representative of a
foreign culture in order to compare and contrast this country's attitudes toward love, honor, and duty. These abstractions would soon
become real enough to the American people as the world edged closer
to another global war.

The biggest hit of the 1938 season, though, was *Brother Rat,* probably because it so faithfully followed the script of the successful
Broadway comedy. Set against the colorful backdrop of Virginia Mili-

**William Tracy braces for a blow at the hands of Wayne Morris while classmates Eddie
Albert and Ronald Reagan look on in this dormitory scene from *Brother Rat* (Warner
Bros., 1938).**

tary Institute, the so-called West Point of the South, the film depends a great deal on the usual military school props and conventions but uses them in such a way as to appear strikingly original in its interpretation—at least for its time. The Keydets' star baseball pitcher, played by Eddie Albert in his original Broadway role, discovers that his life at VMI has become increasingly complicated because of his secret marriage and impending fatherhood. Since marriage prior to graduation is forbidden by the administration, Albert's buddies— played by Ronald Reagan and Wayne Morris—scheme to cover up his predicament until they all can graduate ten weeks later. To complicate the story further, problems arise when Reagan and Morris hide their dates (Jane Wyman and Priscilla Lane) in their quarters. Meanwhile, Albert, who is modeled somewhat after the proverbial dumb athlete, has to find a way to pass chemistry so he can pitch in the big baseball game against one of their biggest rivals, the Virginia Cavaliers. True to the finest tradition of dramatic comedy, all the protagonist's problems are worked out by the graduation ceremonies when Albert finds himself passing out cigars to the chagrined military hierarchy.

Despite this film's delightfully comic perspective, the viewer is occasionally witness to a caustic swipe at the totalitarian tactics of the military system. The movie, much like the play, is really a subtle satire of the military way of life. With the world on the brink of a cataclysmic war that would forever change it, *Brother Rat* stood in the late 1930s as one of the last innocent statements about the military milieu and its psychological effects on the individual. For this reason, viewing this movie today can emphatically point out for us just how much our world has diverged from that of 1938. For an even better understanding of how Hollywood interpreted this expanding gulf, we will now turn to the college-life films of the 1940s to observe how they evolved, reflecting an increasingly critical public consciousness during the 1950s.

3   Extensions: The 1940s–1950s

"That's the trouble . . . too damn many ideas floating
around. . . . You put ideas of any kind into young people's
heads, and the first thing you know, they start believing
them."

—college trustee in James Thurber
and Elliott Nugent's *The Male
Animal* (1940)

"College is a time for making contacts. Meet the people who
can help you when you go out to get a job, and the people
you'll have to deal with if you're in any kind of business. Get
in with a good crowd now, and it'll be easy to keep up with it
after you graduate."

—character in Oakley Hall's
The Corpus of Joe Bailey (1953)

College-life movies produced in the 1940s and 1950s continued to rely
heavily on genre conventions that had been introduced in the 1920s
and diversified in the 1930s. However, these later films occasionally
included some that were critically uncharacteristic of their times even
though they featured all the old familiar trappings. *The Male Animal*
(1942) and *Saturday's Hero* (1951), which will be discussed later in
this section, are both outstanding examples, but it was not until the
late 1950s that Hollywood made a noticeably concerted effort to
question and openly criticize the established system of higher education in this country. As a sign of what was happening on the larger
scene, these later films began to reflect a loss of social innocence and

a break with the traditional values and attitudes that our society had stubbornly clung to for more than a decade after the close of World War II.

With the generally stereotyped service academy movies of the 1920s and 1930s as a prelude, the war years of 1941–45 naturally demanded a more intense, realistic dramatization of real-life situations along with an idealized portrayal of heroic types who could help satisfy the nation's hunger for patriotic inspiration. Although this kind of film entertainment was generally presented in a much more graphic fashion than it was during the 1930s, it was actually nothing more than an extension of that era's special approach to fantasizing experience. In fact, the Hollywood version of World War II showed that patriotic devotion to country could be just as fantasized as most other human endeavors, and today television runs of films like *God Is My Co-Pilot, Stand By for Action,* and *Behind the Rising Sun* clearly demonstrate this point.

Sports, the most popular inspiration for the fantasy background of the college-life movie during the 1930s, extended their popularity on into the next decade, but in the 1940s movie sports drama, the lives of a number of real-life heroes were brought to the screen for war-conditioned audiences whose fantasy needs now required more of a true-to-life flavor. Typically, *Knute Rockne—All-American* (Warner Bros., 1940), which in the words of one highly impressed reviewer was "an inspirational reminder of what this country stands for [and] decidedly timely," patriotically expressed the feeling of the country at the beginning of the 1940s.[1] Carrying on a tradition that had begun in the 1930s, this movie also consecrated the image and reputation of the football coach in the eyes of the American public and in doing so naturally avoided any criticism of the collegiate system itself. Hollywood instinctively recognized that Knute Rockne's self-made life (which was pure Americana in itself), his successful coaching career, and particularly his tragic death at an early age represented the stuff of which great "bio-pics" were made. So, in commemoration of this legendary coach's passing nearly a decade before, and because of the mood of the time, the movie people concluded that the American public was ready for Rockne's story not only as an end in itself but as a special tribute to the American way of life during this critical test of the democratic system.

Like most movies about real people, *Knute Rockne* develops episodically, depicting the biographical facts and events that contributed to the legend of Rockne the man and the coach: his childhood in an immigrant family, working his way through Notre Dame as a superior student and athlete, his love for the game of football and his special role in demonstrating in the 1913 game against Army how the forward pass could revolutionize the sport, his decision to remain at his alma mater as a teacher-coach, his courtship and marriage to his college sweetheart, his unusual success as a coach, and his untimely death in a plane crash in 1931. All these diverse ingredients are held together by a controlling theme and an almost spiritual atmosphere inspired by Rockne's forceful personality and dominant influence on his players. This pervasive spirit underscores the film's basic contention that Rockne's players had become not only better athletes but better men for having dedicated themselves to an ideal. The personal magnetism of Rockne, as well as his strong social presence, is singularly expressed through his close relationship with a talented player like George Gipp (Ronald Reagan) who suddenly dies of pneumonia while still at Notre Dame. (Gipp was supposedly the inspiration for Rockne's famous locker-room pep talk in which he urged his team to "go out and win this one for the Gipper"—an exhortation that has since become fixed in American sports lore.)

In glorifying the college coach as dynamic teacher, father confessor, and intimate friend, Knute Rockne—All-American stood out as one of the few instances where leadership in American higher education had been positively presented in the Hollywood movie. Versatile Pat O'Brien, then at the height of his acting career, turned in an inspired performance as the inimitable Rockne, whom he played so convincingly that he would be permanently associated with the role.[2]

Rockne's screen biography went on to inspire a variety of inferior bio-pics and "spirit" pictures in the 1940s and well into the 1950s. In this pretelevision era, long before the TV medium would make a name like Joe Namath instantly identifiable with both the football field and a consumer product, Hollywood apparently thought that every outstanding college football star who came along was potentially worthy of a movie based on his life, especially during a time when hero types were in great demand.[3] These pictures approached their subject matter in a variety of ways, but they were unanimous in their interpretation of the positive influence of the collegiate experience on their heroes, implying that this source of the indomitable school spirit would inspire these players for the rest of their lives. Actually, the tradition for the "spirit" movies had been established in the 1890s with the appearance of the inspirational school and college fiction written primarily for a youthful audience. In an early scene in The Freshman, before Speedy Lamb leaves home for college, the viewer observes that the impressionable Speedy has been reading about the collegiate exploits of that paragon of fictional athletes, Frank Merriwell. The overall influence of such fiction on the young mind of that day is, of course, incalculable, but its inspirational intent was undoubtedly pervasive enough to have significant impact on the movies' approach to dramatizing collegiate athletic experience.[4]

The crashing impact of an All-American Fullback!

LEW AYRES IN The SPIRIT of NOTRE DAME

with William BAKEWELL · Sally BLANE · J. Farrell McDONALD

THE IMMORTAL
FOUR HORSEMEN

ELMER LAYDEN · JIM CROWLEY
HARRY STUHLDREHER · DON MILLER
and the 7 MULES

LARRY (MOON) MULLINS · JOHN LAW
ADAM WALSH · JOHN J. O'BRIEN
AL HOWARD · ARTHUR McMAHON
"BUCKY" O'CONNOR

with FRANK CARIDEO
of NOTRE DAME

The Notre Dame football mystique inspired one of the earlier school-spirit movies in *The Spirit of Notre Dame* (Universal, 1931).

The war years of the 1940s were dominated by the football teams of the U.S. Military Academy at West Point, and two consensus all-Americans of the period who were chiefly responsible for this predominance were Felix "Doc" Blanchard and Glenn Davis—popularly known as Mr. Inside and Mr. Outside, respectively, in tribute to their assigned running routes on the gridiron. It was only natural, then, that in 1947 a movie of their football exploits would appear. Unfortunately, *The Spirit of West Point* (Film Classics) turned out to be the usual conventionalized version of the military-school athletic experience that audiences had been viewing since the 1920s. Playing themselves, Blanchard and Davis do their best with a sketchy plot that concerns itself mainly with the cadets' personal conflict over whether to turn professional or stay at West Point and earn their commissions. By relying heavily on familiar newsreel footage for scenes of the all-Americans' gridiron achievements, this film loses much of its dramatic intensity. Even assigning popular radio sportscasters Bill Stern, Harry Wismer, and Tom Harmon the task of describing the key games does very little to spark up the action. One only has to observe what the television medium has done to enhance the watching of a college football game to realize how contrived and fantasized this kind of movie is. Displaying a code of honor and standard of behavior that are no longer credible, the "spirit" theme of movies like *The Spirit of West Point* is as old fashioned today as the patriotic mood that inspired it.

The mood did spawn some commendable variations on this theme, though, particularly two about West Point: *Ten Gentlemen from West Point* (20th Century-Fox, 1942) and *The Long Gray Line* (Columbia, 1955). The earlier film concerns itself with the founding of the U.S. Military Academy, a mission which, surprisingly, was not without opposition. With George Montgomery and John Sutton in the lead roles, the plot is built around the selection of ten cadets who are to comprise the academy's first class and the problems they encounter in becoming soldiers of officer rank. The antimilitary group hopes that the toughness of the training will discourage the candidates, but ironically the rigors of the program have a reverse effect on the men with the result that the "spirit" of the academy is born. During the early years of the war, this film was a sure crowd pleaser, particularly in its rousing ending, which paid tribute to the outstanding West Point graduates of the past and present. Once again, in *Ten Gentlemen* we observe the service academy movie's propensity to project its romantic interest through the triangular relationship as Montgomery and Sutton compete for the hand of Maureen O'Hara.

Among the last of the "spirit" movies was John Ford's *The Long Gray Line,* in which Tyrone Power turns in one of his most offbeat performances in the role of Marty Maher, an athletic trainer whose fifty years at West Point have made a legendary figure out of him. The story is told in flashback as the elderly Maher, who wants to stay on at the academy, pleads his case against compulsory retirement before President Eisenhower. The biographical plot highlights the cocky young Irishman's arrival in this country in 1903, his career as an enlisted man at West Point, his boxing ability, which earned him the job of assistant to the athletic director at the academy, and his marriage to an Irish servant girl (appealingly played by Maureen O'Hara). Throughout this film, though, the central focus is on Maher's intensely personal relationship to successive generations of cadets— the "long gray line," which features impressive names like MacArthur, Stilwell, Bradley, Wainwright, and Eisenhower.

The personality of a Marty Maher, as most former collegians will recognize, was representative of the somewhat eccentric but lovable characters that invariably populate the faculty and staff of every American educational institution at some time in its history.[5] Maher's dramatic function as both friend and father figure to the cadets expresses better than anything else in the film the "spirit" that characterizes this kind of movie. As a living example of the dedication to an ideal that his beloved cadets represent, Maher's life, according to this film, was inspired and directed by his experiences at West Point. In fact, the film's main objective appears to be to make viewers realize that the academy itself was Marty Maher's life, and the film ends on an emotional note with the President's approval of Maher's continued tenure, and a dress parade in his honor. *The Long Gray Line* brought a fitting close to an era in which the military-school film had been dominated by the "spirit" theme. With the fading of the patriotic fervor that had expressed itself since the days of World War I, these kinds of movies became rare indeed.

During this period, other bio-pics dramatizing the school-spirit theme and the collegiate experience as highly influential on a central figure concerned themselves with the exploits of well-known athletes who went on to professional sports careers. The more controversial the figure, the more sensational was the promotion copy surrounding the movie based on his life as, for example, the films about Jackie Robinson and Jim Thorpe, which appeared in the early 1950s.[6] De-

Bio-pics like *Jim Thorpe—All American* (Warner Bros., 1951) were permeated with the school-spirit atmosphere. Burt Lancaster played the great Indian athlete from Carlisle College.

spite their varied approaches to filming the biography of a professional athlete, all such movies seem to agree that the collegiate experience has been a forceful one in their subjects' formative years and sufficiently influential to pursue them throughout their lives. Perhaps this sentimental coloration was the fundamental reason that this type of movie never made it big with movie audiences. The reality of athletic competition and the sentiment of personal experience have never mixed too readily on the silver screen, it seems.

During the 1940s and 1950s, before the professional game had actually caught on with sports fans, it was still the collegiate version of football that filled the stadiums around the country. Attesting to this popularity, a couple of appealing movies appeared in the early 1940s that stood out from the usual football tale. Paramount's *The Quarterback* (1940), which had the same title as their 1929 film but a different plot, saw Wayne Morris playing a dual role: exact twins with opposite personalities and habits. As a variation of one of the oldest formulas in dramatic history—the mistaken identity plot—the central situation of this film made for a highly entertaining and amusing story. Morris plays both the studious, well-meaning Jimmy Jones and his athletic bum of a brother, Bill. When the college coach discovers Bill's superior athletic ability, he mistakenly awards brother Jimmy a football scholarship. Like his Harold Lloyd prototype in *The Freshman,* Jimmy doesn't have an ounce of athletic ability but ultimately finds himself playing in the big game. When he is knocked unconscious by the opposition, Bill comes on to take his place and win the game. The picture closes on a happy note, with no one the wiser about their dual identities other than the corner drugstore owner. An important fact contributing to the quality of this film was its excellent supporting cast of character types: Edgar Kennedy, William Frawley, Walter Catlett, Jerome Cowan, and Rod Cameron. The very British Alan Mowbray is cast as a college professor whose fastidious mannerisms helped continue the stereotyping of this familiar character.

The other engaging gridiron caper of the period was *Rise and Shine* (20th Century-Fox, 1941), an hilarious take-off on the intercollegiate football film tradition, with such recognizable genre types as the dumb-ox football player and the eccentric professor as well as the stock events of kidnapping the star player on the eve of the game and, of course, the big game itself. Jack Oakie, looking much too heavy and old by this time to be playing a college football star, is Boley Bolienciewcz, a role obviously inspired by James Thurber's slow-witted athlete of the same name.[7] Having put tiny Clayton College on the football map, Boley is accorded royal treatment by the alumni who want to spread their school's fame by playing Notre Dame. The alumni have made it quite clear to the administration that both Boley's health and grades should be well taken care of. In fact, one of the college's professors, played by the mild-mannered and effete looking Donald Meek, takes Boley into his home to watch over him and see that the prize athlete gets plenty of what he likes most—sleep. Juxtaposing these two familiar types from the Hollywood college-life tradition is a masterly stroke that contributes to some of the film's funniest moments, mainly through the social conflict of natural brute strength and near-genius intelligence. This is a comparison that must have fascinated Thurber, because it is clearly evident in the characters of the athlete and the academician that he so vividly portrayed in his play, *The Male Animal* (the film version of which will be discussed later in this chapter). The Thurber source piece for *Rise and Shine* is drawn on directly when Boley comes up for an examination in economics and has difficulty in naming a mode of transportation, but when he is asked what he does to stay in shape, his reply of "train" rates a pass on the exam. Thurber's satirical portrait of the college football player reveals his obvious distaste for a type he undoubtedly looked upon as a lower form of life.

Recognizing the Clayton team as a good betting choice, a New York mobster (Sheldon Leonard) decides to send some of his henchmen along with one of his nightclub performers (George Murphy) out to the college town to spy on Boley's physical condition before every game. By the time of the big game with Notre Dame, mob leader Leonard determines that he can win more money by betting against Clayton, currently a strong favorite because of Boley, who is now looked upon as one of football's all-time players. In order to keep him out of the game, Leonard has Boley kidnapped. Of course, Boley is rescued in time to play, none the worse for his abduction ordeal except for having been kept up all night. At this point, Murphy turns out to be the real hero of the story when, after telling Boley that a nearby dam has burst, the sleepy halfback awakes to run ninety-five yards for the winning touchdown. In fact, Boley not only scores a touchdown, he runs clear out of the stadium in his search for higher ground. With additional comedic support from Milton Berle and Walter Brennan, *Rise and Shine* was a pleasant romp for most audiences, who appreciated what this film did with the overly familiar character types and stock events of the collegiate movie.

As a portent of things to come, though, some movies of this era began to take a more serious turn in their treatment of the collegiate athletic experience. For example, *Yesterday's Heroes* (20th Century-Fox, 1940) zeroed in on the commercialization of college football and its powerful sway over those who participate in it. Robert Sterling plays a serious student who is more interested in pursuing a medical career than in playing football, but his personal plans are dashed when he finds himself pressured into devoting most of his time to the gridiron fortunes of his school rather than to his own professional goals. A unique visual technique is used to reveal Sterling's story by having him look through his scrapbook of football achievements while his personal decline to the present low point in his life is shown in flashback. The handsome Sterling, one of the more promising movie finds of the 1940s, never really made it big, but he did manage to turn in an outstanding performance in this, his finest film.

It wasn't until 1951 that the most critical film ever made of college football appeared. *Saturday's Hero* (Columbia) assumed a serious stance that was enhanced by two important factors: the quality acting of its lead performers, and the realism of its football action scenes. In stark contrast to the "spirit" movies that glorified football as a character-building sport and the coach as an exemplary and honorable man, this film pointed out all the shortcomings of a system that had evolved into big business.

John Derek plays Steve Novak, son of immigrant parents, whose sensational career as a high-school football player wins him a scholarship to a tradition-bound but athletically ambitious southern university. Idealistic and studious, Steve believes that attending a school

In *Saturday's Hero* (Columbia, 1951), football player John Derek is told the bad news that an injury has terminated his playing career. Derek's sponsor Sidney Blackmer, newspaperman Elliott Lewis, and his coach Otto Hulett look on.

like Jackson will elevate him above his humble background to an acceptable social and cultural standing. Unlike most Hollywood athletic heroes, education is foremost with Steve Novak while football is just a means to an end. But soon the realities of the collegiate system undermine his ideals as Steve is personally transformed through his sobering introduction to the snobbish fraternity system, his shocking awakening to his fellow players' sarcastic attitude toward school spirit, and his growing realization that he is nothing more than a piece of merchandise bought and paid for by the system. Intensely dedicated to his studies at first and inspired by his English professor, who ironically types all football players as stupid, Steve soon makes only mediocre grades due to the inordinate amount of time he must devote to the football program.[8] This part of Steve's life at college is graphically brought to the screen as his slave-driving coach (Otto Hulett) puts Steve and his teammates through brutally endless scrimmages.

In the meantime Steve has fallen in love with the niece (Donna Reed) of a wealthy alumnus (Sidney Blackmer) who is one of the driving forces behind Jackson University's rise as a football power. In fact, it is he who has put up the money in behalf of Steve's scholarship, so his attitude toward his protégé approaches that of a slavemaster from the old South. This relationship is one that the film makes the most of to put across Steve Novak's ironic predicament. After Blackmer attempts to break up the romance between Steve and his niece, Steve's dreams of a better life are finally shattered by a career-ending injury, and one of the film's most affective scenes shows the injured player limping down the stadium tunnel to the dressing room, the crowd noise still ringing in his ears. In an atypically bleak ending for this kind of movie, Steve returns home to an ordinary job and night school, all the while anticipating a reunion with his girl. When contrasted with the generally optimistic tenor of the times, this film's grittily realistic outlook makes it unique in many respects. From a technical standpoint, too, *Saturday's Hero* made a clean break with convention by scrapping newsreel footage altogether and filming some of the most savagely realistic football action scenes ever seen in the collegiate film. Through its marriage of theme and technical achievement, *Saturday's Hero* goes beyond the conventions of the football drama to visualize what happens when the American dream fails.

The influence of the 1930s football melodrama still lingered, however, and even though *The All-American* (Universal-International, 1953) tried hard to be serious, it ultimately failed in its intent because of its overreliance on stock situations. Nevertheless, when accepted for what it is, this movie does come across as fairly entertaining. Tony Curtis, whose parents were killed en route to see him play, has quit football only to be lured back to the game because of his cocksure manner and exceptional playing ability. Due to certain problems created by his encounter with the school's snob element—yet another variation on *The Freshman* theme—Curtis is expelled on the day of the big game only to find himself reinstated in time to win the game in the last quarter. This film was produced and directed by two former University of Southern California all-Americans: Aaron Rosenberg (1933) and Jesse Hibbs (1927), a combination that may account for the sympathetic, crowd-pleasing interpretation of Curtis's Frank Merriwell–type role. The customary display of collegiate pulchritude comes through in Lori Nelson as Curtis's understanding girl friend and Mamie Van Doren as a sexy Lorelei who lures the players to her off-limits tavern. The practice of featuring name personalities from the real-life football world was extended with the appearances of Herman Hickman, Frank Gifford, and Tom Harmon—all of whom would go on in television to help condition the general public's feeling for sports as a form of entertainment.[9]

The familiar situation of the school about to be closed down if its mortgage isn't paid on time crops up again in *Trouble Along the Way* (Warner Brothers, 1953). In this version, John Wayne, a renegade ex-coach who has seen better days, is approached by the rector (Charles Coburn) of a catholic college called St. Anthony's and offered the head coaching job. Coburn is as dedicated and idealistic as most movie priests, and according to formula, holds the conviction that the school can be bailed out of economic difficulty if it can come up with a winning football team. Admitting to having been "kicked out of the Big Ten, the Ivy League, and the Southern Conference," Wayne flatly refuses the position at St. Anthony's but later accepts in order to get his young daughter into a wholesome environment. It seems that Coach Wayne's private life is fraught with certain problems that are more challenging than any he has had to confront on the gridiron. Charged with the neglect of his daughter by his ex-wife, Wayne is directed by the court to report periodically to a probation officer (played by Donna Reed) with whom he eventually falls in love. In the meantime Wayne has turned out a winning football team, but when his unscrupulous recruiting methods come to light, Coburn disbands the team for the sake of the school's good name. Wayne's private life fares much better, though, with his problems with his ex-wife resolved, his daughter's lot improved, and his romance with Miss Reed obviously headed for the altar. With its novel twist to the usual ending of a football drama and its stress on real human concerns, *Trouble Along the Way* was indicative of a change in the wind as movie audiences grew receptive to a more realistic approach to tried-and-true subject matter. By the middle of the 1950s, the conventional football movie, along with the school-spirit theme, was becoming a part of the Hollywood past.

Charles Coburn is a priest who cajoles ex-coach John Wayne into coaching a catholic school football team already "at the bottom of the Ivy League barrel" in *Trouble Along the Way* (Warner Bros., 1953).

In the meantime, the collegiate musical was still thriving and expressing itself in various ways that still came across as extensions of the prototypal Hollywood musical of the 1930s. In 1947, MGM came up with one of the season's hits when it remade the 1930 version of *Good News*. With new songs added to the original score created by the team of Lew Brown, B. G. De Sylva, and Ray Henderson, *Good News* turned out to be good entertainment, good satire, and good box office. Perhaps the influx of returning veterans to our colleges and universities had something to do with the upsurge of interest in the college-life musical at that time, but whatever the nostalgic inspiration, *Good News* appeared to have a lot of fun with the familiar conventions of the collegiate caper that had been established in the social-minded 1920s. There was the triangular romance situation with pert June Allyson and comely Patricia Marshall vying for the affections of football star Peter Lawford, who tries to impress the girls that he is not only athletic but rich. True to formula, Lawford becomes ineligible to play in the big game when he flunks his French exam. We discover, however, that he has actually failed on purpose because he had promised to marry Miss Marshall if he wins the big game. Of course, it is Miss Allyson he's really interested in, and she reciprocates her interest in Lawford when she sees to it that his grade is restored in time for him to come back and win the big game in the final three minutes. To cap things off, Miss Marshall, who has found out by now that her football hero is not the rich boy she thought he was, turns him down, and all ends well for everybody concerned. Featuring solid, captivating tunes like the title song, "The Best Things in Life Are Free," "Lucky in Love," and "Varsity Drag," *Good News* came across in the best tradition of the technicolor MGM musical. Among the pleasant surprises that contributed to the popularity of the musical numbers was the song-and-dance talent of Peter Lawford in his first starring role.

While this appealing movie helped perpetuate the fantasy side of the college experience for a new generation unfamiliar with the likes of a 1930s musical, it was fairly obvious to both old and young moviegoers that MGM was the champion producer of musicals of all types, and that the MGM musical production had the power to transport the viewer to a fantasy world peculiarly this studio's own. Two widely popular MGM musicals with a collegiate theme that readily qualify in this respect were *Girl Crazy* (1943) and *Bathing Beauty* (1944).

During the 1940s, MGM revived the college-life musical with *Good News* (1947). Here, June Allyson and Peter Lawford lead the student body in a rousing rendition of "Varsity Drag."

Spotlighting the magnificent music of George Gershwin, the big-band interpretations of Tommy Dorsey and his orchestra, and the dynamic acting, singing, and dancing team of Mickey Rooney and Judy Garland, *Girl Crazy* had too much going for it to be hampered by the familiar plot devices it had inherited from the dozens of college-life musicals that preceded it. The story is built around a rich newspaper publisher's efforts to settle down his girl-chasing son (Mickey Rooney) by sending him to an all-male college in a remote part of Arizona. A romance blossoms anyway when Mickey meets the granddaughter (Judy Garland) of the college dean—played by long-time character actor, Guy Kibbee. When the student body learns that the college is to be shut down because of a decrease in enrollment, Mickey and Judy, in their usual resourceful fashion, head up a campaign to put on a rodeo featuring musical numbers with a hundred dancing collegians, an event designed to bring national attention to the college and boost enrollment sufficiently to keep the school open.

As he had in three previous Rooney-Garland musicals, Busby Berkeley directed the musical numbers, lending them his distinctive flair for originality, particularly in the rousing finale of "I've Got Rhythm." In fact, the Berkeley touch was never better, and, of course, the movie's familiar plot is helped along by it. Mickey's relationship with Judy becomes strained when, for publicity purposes, he chooses the governor's daughter as queen of the rodeo. But Mickey's tactics turn out sound, for after the big show school applications start pouring in, causing Judy to see Mickey and his enterprising ways in a new light. Based on the 1930 Broadway musical, *Girl Crazy* drew on a favorite plot device of the college-life movie—how to get the economically unsound school back on an even keel. At a time when our schools are finding it increasingly difficult to balance their budgets, this theme is ironically still timely. Considering the outright competition for students that exists today, college public relations offices would probably concur that the publicity stunts of a movie-world Mickey Rooney are really not so far-fetched after all.

Mainly because of its spectacular water settings and coordinated swimming and diving routines, *Bathing Beauty* had even more going for it from an audience point of view than did *Girl Crazy*. Starring Red Skelton, one of the most popular comics of this period, and shapely Esther Williams, whose looks matched her swimming skills, this film introduced the visually appealing water ballet to moviegoers. Judging from audiences' enthusiastic reaction, it was as revolutionary as anything they had ever seen on the screen. In contrast to the exciting visual effects, the film's skimpy plot is based on college girl Williams's romance with songwriter Skelton, who, in chasing after his dream girl, carries on a running feud with collegiate rules and regulations. Echoing the Rooney-Garland team efforts, Miss Williams's

Girl Crazy (MGM, 1943) had Mickey Rooney and Judy Garland cavorting in a collegiate setting out West, backed up by the music of Tommy Dorsey and his orchestra.

ability in the swimming pool and Skelton's talent for turning out popular tunes help put an unknown college on the map. Beyond its attempt to project a story line, though, *Bathing Beauty* functions as a showcase for some of the MGM lot's most memorable and awe-inspiring visual exhibitions, climaxing with a grandiose water pageant in which Miss Williams's aquatic talents come through in crowd-pleasing style. As though all this were not enough, the film features the orchestral renditions of Harry James and Xavier Cugat, as well as the flashy organ stylings of Ethel Smith. Obviously, the inspiration for the college-life musical was still very much alive in the 1940s. A contemporary reviewer went so far as to call *Bathing Beauty* "one of the finest filmusicals ever made" and a movie from which Esther Williams emerges as a "full-fledged star," not just because of her swimming skills but due to her natural acting ability.[10]

In 1940, another female performer with even more long-range potential in both the movies and television was enhancing her star image in a college-life musical called *Too Many Girls* (RKO). Her name was Lucille Ball, and in heading a cast that included Richard Carlson, Eddie Bracken, Frances Langford, Ann Miller, and future husband

Desi Arnaz, she displayed her special flair for light comedy. Derived directly from producer George Abbott's Broadway hit and its Rodgers-Hart score, this movie had a plot somewhat reminiscent of *Girl Crazy* in reverse. Lucy is a rich girl whose father sends her off to college in a remote area of the Southwest and hires four football players to act as her bodyguards. The school's football team is too distracted by the numerous co-eds to win many games, but when Lucy's gridiron guards are persuaded to join the team, the school suddenly finds itself a winner in the national limelight. All those girls aren't so bad either; in addition to inspiring the players, they contribute a great deal to the staging of some fast-moving, colorful musical sequences, especially the final production number featuring Desi Arnaz doing his speciality version of the conga. With its thematic musical numbers interspersed between a conventional football story and Lucy's romancing of Richard Carlson, *Too Many Girls* is a film cut right out of the 1930s collegiate pattern, its prime virtue being the assignment of Miss Ball to one of her better musical roles.[11]

The Hollywood version of the collegiate experience, whether in the form of melodrama, comedy, or the musical, was still a very appealing source of entertainment to the young moviegoer of the 1940s, and the moviemakers of the time—particularly those associated with the B movie studios—were highly sensitive to the social impact of college life on the youthful mind. In fact, collegiate movies designed for a young audience continued to appear well into the 1960s, when the rapidly expanding medium of television made them obsolete, forcing Hollywood to search for more sensational social themes and subject matter for the more sophisticated and critically demanding moviegoers of the later 1960s. Nevertheless, the affective powers of these earlier films should not be underrated, for it is apparent, though impossible to measure statistically, that their overall influence was considerable on youthful perception, behavior, and life-styles. One can't help but wonder just how many young people of the 1935 to 1950 era were inspired to go on to college because of a rollicking, fast-paced B movie they might have seen—movies like *Campus Rhythm,* *Let's Go Collegiate,* and *Betty Co-ed.* By the same token, one might wonder just how many of these same young people had their fondest dreams dashed when they discovered that their real-life experiences at college failed to meet the expectations that the movie dream had promised. The formula for the class B musical, with its focus on the social importance of the individual and his or her ability to overcome whatever might prevent the achievement of social success and popularity, was one that measured the optimistic outlook of young people against the problems of growing up in a world where the odds appeared to be stacked against them.

A number of outstanding B movies exemplified this attitude. One of the most entertaining was Columbia's *Sweetheart of the Campus* (1941), yet another story about a school with financial problems but with a uniquely different twist. When bandleader Ozzie Nelson, playing himself, prepares to open his new nightclub near the campus of Lambert Tech, he, his band, and his featured singer (Ruby Keeler) are arrested under an old law forbidding any night spot to operate within five miles of the campus. The arrests have been spearheaded by the bluenose daughter of the college's founder, but she is countermanded by the college president's daughter (Harriet Hilliard) in still another version of the "college widow" theme. Because the enrollment at Lambert has dwindled to only about a hundred, Harriet sets out to find a way to attract students, even if it means sacrificing studies and accepting swing music, a style very popular with the youth of the time. Meanwhile, the straitlaced founder's daughter seeks to enforce a provision of her mother's will stating that the college property will revert to her if at least three hundred students fail to pass their courses with a grade of *B*. But the opportunistic Harriet, who by now has fallen for Ozzie, enrolls him and his band at Lambert with the unique idea of turning the college gym into a night club—such an action would get around the five-mile statute because the club would be *on* campus rather than *near* it. In no time at all, enrollment begins to climb, and even an entire football squad registers. As a natural crowd-pleaser for the young, *Sweetheart of the Campus* set out to demonstrate that education and good times complemented each other.[12]

Other quality B musicals of the 1940s that relied on a socially oriented theme for audience appeal were *Sis Hopkins* (Republic, 1941) and *Betty Co-ed* (Columbia, 1947). The former film starred comedienne Judy Canova as a country bumpkin attending a snobbish girls' school, where the classic collegiate conflict of natural innocence and a sophisticated system again takes place. The rural type was a familiar role for Miss Canova. In this one, as in all her others, she manages to get the upper hand in the end, but not without a lot of laughs along the way, attributable both to her comedic talents and those of the irrepressible Jerry Colonna.[13]

Betty Co-ed, with Jean Porter in the title role, had a serious side. This film attempted to expose the elitism of the sorority system—a topic that would take on increasing interest in the years ahead. When Miss Porter's background as a carnival girl is laid bare by her uppity sorority sisters, she turns the tables on them by becoming the most popular girl on campus through her naturally winning manner and her singing talent. (One of her songs in this film, "Put the Blame on Mame," became a big hit during the 1940s.) Creditable acting support is supplied by Jackie Moran, one of the youth stars of the era, and Edward van Sloan as a college teacher, but it is Jean Porter who steals the show to make *Betty Co-ed* a surprisingly good low-budget musical, proving that some B movie efforts could compete successfully with the more lavish productions of the bigger studios.[14]

Since the 1940s, an astounding growth in enrollment has taken place in our institutions of higher learning, which has just recently begun to subside after peaking in the 1960s. A most significant contributing factor to the burgeoning of campus enrollments, of course, has been society's evaluation of the college degree's worth in the marketplace. In other words, the underlying reason for attending college during this period was not so much to pursue knowledge as it was to qualify for a good-paying job. Accordingly, the continuing democratization of American higher education created opportunities for many persons who otherwise would never have set foot on a college campus. The most far-reaching of these educational opportunities was promulgated after World War II in a public law known popularly as the G.I. Bill, which enabled returning servicemen to obtain a college education at government expense. The unique social conditions created by the large influx of veterans who took advantage of the bill's benefits—resulting in campus housing shortages, married couples with children living on campus, maturity versus youth in the classroom, and a variety of other unusual situations—inspired a number of films. These ranged from the serious drama, *Apartment for Peggy* (20th Century-Fox, 1948), to the appealing musical, *Yes Sir, That's My Baby* (Universal-International, 1949), both films in their way representative of the transformation of the collegiate atmosphere through the ubiquitous presence of the returning veteran.

In *Yes Sir, That's My Baby,* one of the most unusual triangular situations of the college-life film is built around the experience of an ex-G.I. (Donald O'Connor), his wife (Gloria DeHaven) and child, and the game of football. Against his wife's wishes, O'Connor mobilizes his G.I. classmates to play football for dear old Granger U. After a series of obligatory musical interludes and the futile attempts of a prototypal women's rights crusader to thwart the men's plans to play football, the guys naturally win both the right to play and the big game in the final seconds. Charles Coburn shows up again as a collegiate type, this time as a biology professor who doubles as football coach, as this was a time when specialized positions were difficult to fill. Inspiring a couple of imaginative musical production numbers, the male-female clash of this film looks ahead some twenty years to a more troubled era when the children of these "campus families" would be staging their own crusade for individual rights—but in a much more dramatic fashion.

The title of this movie reflects the period's nostalgia for the 1920s, which began with the 1947 version of *Good News*. The trend was still going strong in 1953 when a musical interpretation of writer Max

Donald O'Connor, a G.I. Bill student, must choose between football or his family in *Yes, Sir, That's My Baby* (Universal-International, 1949). Charles Coburn is his coach and Gloria DeHaven, his wife.

Shulman's conception of the typical college man appeared—*The Affairs of Dobie Gillis* (MGM). Destined to become a hit television series, *Dobie Gillis* had a contemporary setting, though most of the song-and-dance sequences relied on the tunes of an earlier era. While singing and dancing to nostalgic numbers like "All I Do Is Dream Of You," Bobby Van and Debbie Reynolds make an attractive college couple involved in the problems of young love. What plot there is concerns itself with the generation gap between young people and their parents as well as with the continuing feud between students and the educational establishment. Hans Conried plays a fussy English professor, and functions as a symbol of the collegiate system's artificial airs, which contrast markedly with the students' natural attitudes toward life—still another version of the basic conflict that underlies all college-oriented movies.

The 1930s era was still very much in evidence in more than just a nostalgic sense, as witnessed by the remakes of several prototypal collegiate films. In 1942, Paramount came out with *Sweater Girl*, a musical version of *College Scandal* (1935). With a variety of settings displaying plenty of pretty girls, the later film adheres closely to the original plot. Befuddled Eddie Bracken plays the role of the college student bent on solving two campus murders while his fellow students are putting together their annual musical show (which naturally allows for the introduction of the film's musical numbers). In fact, the highlight of this picture is the Jule Styne–Frank Loesser score, which includes one of the most popular songs of the war years: "I Don't Want to Walk Without You." This film's mixture of comedy, mystery, and music was handled so skillfully that one reviewer was moved to comment that *Sweater Girl* was exceptional in its avoidance of the "usual artificiality of college pictures" and therefore contained the "spark of reality."[15]

In 1952, Warner Brothers remade its popular 1938 movie *Brother Rat* as a musical and called it *About Face.* Starring singer Gordon McRae and the ebullient Eddie Bracken, this version stuck reasonably close to the original story wherein three cadets at a southern military school try to buck the regulations of the institution, with some amusing results. Although the original story line lost something in translation, *About Face* profited from the talents of newcomer Joel

Bobby Van and Barbara Ruick register concern over Debbie Reynolds's chemistry lab experiment in *The Affairs of Dobie Gillis* **(MGM, 1953).**

Grey and the appealing Phyllis Kirk as the girl who is secretly married to one of the cadets.[16]

In 1950 Warner Brothers came up with a military school musical that appeared to be a synthesis of two of their finest musicals of the 1930s: *Flirtation Walk* and *Varsity Show.* This latest production was called *The West Point Story,* and it starred James Cagney as a fading Broadway director who accepts the assignment to head up the annual "100th Night" show at West Point. We learn that there is more to his mission than just that of directing the big show, however. It seems that the book and music of the show have been written by a cadet (Gordon MacRae) whose producer uncle thinks that the material is good enough for Broadway. Cagney's real job, then, is to persuade cadet MacRae to quit West Point and strike out for Broadway. Absurdly enough, the plot has Cagney entering the academy as a cadet and therefore subject to its regulations during the time that he tries to come up with a way to cajole MacRae into leaving. Cagney, of course, is his usual buoyant and effervescent self, while Virginia Mayo and Doris Day lend sufficient feminine interest to offset the natural male dominance of a military-school film. MacRae and Miss

The military school musical of the 1930s lived on in *The West Point Story* (Warner Bros., 1950), starring James Cagney. Gordon MacRae is to Cagney's extreme left, and Alan Hale, Jr. is directly behind.

Day are assigned the bulk of the Jule Styne–Sammy Cahn songs, and the dance routines fall to Gene Nelson. The dramatic highlight of the movie is contained in the confrontation between Cagney's forceful personality and the authority of the academy, with the irrepressible Cagney getting the edge. An unusually long film for its kind, *The West Point Story* comes across as a curious blend of forced plot, musical extravaganza, and the old "spirit" movie that originated in the 1930s. In 1950, moviegoers had not yet lost their feel for this sort of thing, but the Korean conflict (which began in the same year) would in time help them reshape their thinking about the interrelationship of war and political posture.

As a cadet who must keep his real identity a secret, James Cagney performed a role in *The West Point Story* that was another favorite plot device of the collegiate film. In *How to Be Very, Very Popular* (20th Century-Fox, 1955), a remake of 1934's *She Loves Me Not,* the mistaken identity situation was carried to its farcical limits.[17] In taking some liberties with the original plot, this movie tells the story of two girlie-show performers—Stormy Tornado (Betty Grable) and Curly Flagg (Sheree North). Having witnessed the murder of a fellow entertainer, these two escape the killer's clutches to hide out in a college fraternity house, much to the delight of three of the house's occupants—Robert Cummings, Tommy Noonan, and Orson Bean. They find a way to hide the girls from the administration, since it is against school regulations—certainly for this time—to mix sexes in the dorms and the frat houses. A series of screwball comedy incidents such as the accidental hypnotizing of Curly (she goes into a dance routine whenever she hears the word "salomy"), the girls' attempts to avoid the murderer's threats, and the wild police pursuit of the suspect precipitate the movie's wacky climax when the culprit is captured during commencement ceremonies. Nunally Johnson was script writer, director, and producer of this film, which continued to reflect the perennial social concern of the college-life movie both by the social relationship of its principals to the collegiate scene and by the ironic connotation of its title. The quest for peer popularity was still foremost among collegians at this time, as was the running feud between the students and the administration. The prevalent concerns of the administration are evident, too, when perennial administrator-professor type Charles Coburn, cast here as the college president, blusters that he'd "graduate a three-headed goat for a million dollars." In the college-life film, the administration's search for a bigger endowment is as intense as the students' search for popular identity.

In *She's Working Her Way through College* (Warner Brothers, 1952), Virginia Mayo, like Misses Grable and North, is a lady of burlesque but one who elects to go to college to improve her chances of becoming a famous writer. Billed on the stage as "Hot Garters

Gertie, the Anatomy Award Winner," Miss Mayo is compelled to assume a more socially acceptable identity lest her plans be quashed at the outset. Her situation contributes to the basic dramatic conflict of this movie—democratic naturalness versus patrician snobbery and pretense, another variation of the collegiate movie's favorite theme. When Miss Mayo's stripper background is revealed, the chairman of the college's board of trustees (Roland Winters) takes action to have her expelled. He demands that one of her professors, played by Ronald Reagan, read the expulsion statement before the student body. Instead, Reagan tears up the speech, declaring that to expel Miss Mayo would be undemocratic and against the basic principles of this country. In the eyes of the students the professor is an instant hero, and Miss Mayo, fearful that Reagan will lose his job, confronts chairman Winters and discovers that he is a woman-chaser who once tried to put the make on her during her stripper days. Naturally, Winters's hands are now tied and he has to submit to Miss Mayo's wishes, which include a promotion for Reagan and her right to remain in school. Loosely based on *The Male Animal* (Warner Bros., 1942), this film was one of the few musicals that managed to get across a serious point in an entertaining fashion. Coming in for equal shares of the satirical brunt of this picture are the usual ingredients of the collegiate film: the campus football hero (Gene Nelson), the former all-American (Don DeFore) who can't forget he was once a big star, and the youthful escapades of college life. However, a refreshing element of *She's Working Her Way through College* is its concentration on the human interest side of a college professor.

By the 1940s, the image of the college professor in the movies had received generally spotty interpretation, as we have observed in a number of cases. As a character type whose dedication to the world of ideas contradicts the American bent for the practical side of experience, the college professor in the movies was a natural for comic portraiture. *The Male Animal,* one of the première comedy plays and films of the 1940s, did the most for improving public sympathy for the college professor. This production resulted from the combined efforts of James Thurber and Elliott Nugent. Nugent was a versatile force of the American stage and film who had acquired considerable experience within the college-life movie genre as a playwright (*The Poor Nut),* an actor (*So This Is College),* and director (*She Loves Me Not).* It was fitting, then, that he was assigned to direct *The Male Animal.* His assignment undoubtedly accounted for this film's realistic tone within an atmosphere of comedy. On the other hand, James Thurber must have drawn on his experiences as a student at Ohio State in contributing his sharp satirical edge to the characters themselves.

In both the play and the film version the script stands as a perceptive and penetrating satire of the conflict between individual princi-

An ill-at-ease Ronald Reagan, playing a college professor, finds himself in the spotlight during Virginia Mayo's burlesque routine in *She's Working Her Way through College* (Warner Bros., 1952).

ples and the power of a system. Of course, this conflict had been the inspiration of many a collegiate film's dramatic sense, but never before had it been so forcefully presented, especially in a comedy. Like Ronald Reagan in the musical variation of this story *(She's Working Her Way through College),* Henry Fonda is a professor dedicated to the cause of academic freedom, whose job is threatened by the witch-hunting tactics of the college board of trustees, chaired by Eugene Pallette. Among the most talented of Hollywood's character actors,

Pallette delivers one of his best performances as the bigoted and narrow-minded individual who stands for everything that the idealistic Fonda is against. Even the security of Fonda's marriage to Olivia DeHavilland is undermined by the appearance of her former college boy friend, a one-time all-American football player (Jack Carson) who delights in putting down the high-minded notions of Fonda through a crude, animalistic interpretation of experience. The film's story, following the lead of its title, suggests that there are two basic types of males—the brain and the jock—symbolized by the roles of Fonda and Carson and their inevitable clash.

Ironically, though, it is Professor Fonda who resorts to primitive tactics to beat the athlete at his own game. He not only wins the reassurance of his wife and the faith of his students in his championing of the right to teach freely, he wins over the audience, too, by his first-rate performance. While this film's satirical bite is directed at all the familiar trappings of the collegiate experience—the elitist fraternity system, the liberal-thinking student, big-game football rallies, the overly-adulated athletic hero, and, of course, the blind, authoritarian methods of the administration and its board of trustees— its comically heroic portrait of the college professor is exceptional in

Professor Henry Fonda's stand on academic freedom makes him an instant hero to his students in *The Male Animal* (Warner Bros., 1942). The film also starred Olivia De-Havilland (left) and Joan Leslie (right).

the annals of the collegiate film genre. A first-rate script and excellent cast (featuring Fonda's superb acting talent) combined in *The Male Animal* to produce a film whose message went beyond our usual expectations of the college-life movie to tell us something meaningful about the human condition. Relying on the microcosm of the college campus to make their comments, Thurber and Nugent explored an area that would inspire the thematic approach and serious intent of many collegiate films to follow.

Generally speaking, though, most positive characterizations of the college teacher role were drawn after the sentimental model of the British schoolmaster of *Goodbye, Mr. Chips,* an image whose human side overshadowed the affairs of the classroom to emphasize the affairs of the heart. MGM's *Forty Little Mothers* (1940), in which Eddie Cantor plays a professor at an all-girls' school, is a case in point. Because he is a stern taskmaster in the classroom, the students do not take to Cantor at first. When they find out that he is harboring an abandoned baby in his quarters, they feel they've come up with a way to have him kicked off the faculty because of a campus rule against this sort of thing. However, upon confronting the cute little tyke, the girls—forty of them led by spunky Bonita Granville—find their maternal instincts severely tested and begin to aid Cantor in his secret task. When the administration discovers what's going on, Professor Cantor is dismissed, but the girls threaten to revolt and the administration accedes to their demands. Cantor retains his job, the girls go back to class, and even the baby's delinquent mother shows up. Directed by Busby Berkeley, who occasionally lent his special touch to films other than musicals, *Forty Little Mothers* demonstrated that Eddie Cantor, better known for his comedy leads in some innocuous musicals of the 1930s, could make the most of a rather thin dramatic situation.

One of the more delightful comedies built around the problems of a professorial type was *The Trouble with Women* (Paramount, 1947) in which Ray Milland is a psychology professor with some explicit theories about the treatment of women in particular and the relationship of the sexes in general at a time when the women's liberation movement wasn't even a glimmer of an idea in the minds of most women. As the author of a controversial book which contends that women prefer to be treated rough by their men, Milland sues a newspaper for a large sum of money when he is quoted out of context. This action prompts the paper's editor (Brian Donlevy) to send out his star girl reporter (Teresa Wright) to Milland's college to try to smooth things out. Naturally, she proceeds to fall in love with Professor Milland, who turns out to be not nearly as tough as his exterior would suggest. In delineating a character variation that would eventually evolve in the 1970s into the austere and caustic Professor Charles

Kingsfield of *The Paper Chase,* the movies were finally beginning to interpret the academic type in a three-dimensional light.[18]

Even so, some movies of the 1940s still persisted in presenting the stereotype of the college professor as brilliant but eccentric and impractical, as in the examples of Ray Milland in *It Happens Every Spring* (20th Century-Fox, 1949) and Fred MacMurray in *Family Honeymoon* (Universal-International, 1948).[19] Neither of these films can be strictly called a collegiate movie, but the latter film is worth a closer look for its rendering of the academic character as typically unsuited for romance and the realistic demands of married life. When biology professor Fred MacMurray marries a widow (Claudette Colbert) with three children, the basis for a broad farcical situation is set up by MacMurray's inability to meet the essential needs of a ready-made family. Playing a scholar "more familiar with botanical behaviorism" than with the behavior patterns of children, MacMurray pulls off another of his pleasantly befuddled, crowd-pleasing performances as we watch his honeymoon with both wife and children turn into a misadventure that is nothing short of disastrous. Described by New York newspaper critic Lee Mortimer as "superior comedy," *Family Honeymoon* looks ahead to the television situation comedy series of the 1950s, which Mr. MacMurray himself would play a big part in developing. His hilarious bouts with the three cantankerous juveniles of *Family Honeymoon* must have provided him with some solid experience for his switch to the popular TV series "My Three Sons." If we were to take seriously MacMurray's role in *Family Honeymoon,* though, we would certainly conclude that the college professor was a miserable failure as a family man.[20]

The woman academician was not spared either. The paradox of the brilliant academic specialist knowing very little about love and human nature was expressed through the role of a woman dean in Columbia's *A Woman of Distinction* (1950) with fairly entertaining results, due mainly to the film's excellent cast. In the title role, Rosalind Russell plays Susan Middlecott, dean of Benton College, a distinguished school for women. Supremely dedicated to her career and to the welfare of her adopted daughter, Dean Middlecott has made it frigidly clear that she has "no room for romance" in her life. However, when she meets visiting professor Alec Stevenson (Ray Milland in yet another collegiate role), some of the snow begins to melt as she finds herself attracted to him. The attraction is mutual, and soon Professor Stevenson even expresses his intentions of marrying her but realizes that he has quite a task before him in trying to convince the dean that marriage can be more vital to her life than a career. When a campus scandal threatens over the contested legitimacy of the dean's daughter, Stevenson chivalrously defends her. Ultimately, matters are cleared up, though somewhat in the manner of a screw-

In *The Trouble with Women* (Paramount, 1947), professor Ray Milland is the author of a book that argues for the superiority of men over women. Before it's all over, though, Teresa Wright has Milland eating out of the palm of her hand.

ball comedy, when the lady dean decides that it wouldn't be such a bad idea after all to sacrifice her career and marry the good professor. To the audience, the film's main intent appeared to be the revelation that academic types are real people with problems and concerns like anyone else.[21] The times were certainly ripe for the development of this kind of attitude, for by the 1950s college campuses across the country were beginning to overflow with students, and moviegoers were becoming more receptive to humanized portraits of academic types and more realistic views of their relationships with students.

Certainly, in *Teacher's Pet* (Paramount, 1958), the stereotype of the woman academician as a sexless, cloistered drudge is appealingly reversed when a crusty, hard-boiled New York newspaper editor (Clark Gable) falls head over heels in love with a pretty Columbia journalism instructor (Doris Day). Invited to present a lecture in Miss Day's class—although they have never met—Gable refuses on the grounds that one learns the newspaper profession through experience and not in the classroom. But after he sees Miss Day, Gable readily revises his outlook and even enrolls in her class under a pseudonym.

The situation of the veteran newspaperman hiding his professional identity in order to perform as a student and get closer to Miss Day establishes the comedic tone of this movie. On a more serious side, Gable's attitude toward the process of education, in particular to the teaching of journalism ("amateurs teaching amateurs how to be amateurs," he comments at one point), reflects the basic feeling of the self-made type in America, and its suspicion of the formal educational system. Substantiating Gable's prejudices in a satirical sense is the role played by Gig Young, who as Gable's rival for Miss Day's affections stands for all the things that Gable is against—particularly intellectual pretense and gobbledygook. The fact that Young plays the part of a psychologist who is also a successful author of books that advance new, revolutionary social ideas reinforces Gable's stance and points to the field of psychology as the most vulnerable and susceptible academic subject area for satire in the college-life movie. In one of the better performances of his later years, Gable manages to win out over the affectations of Young in the end, but in the process learns to temper his own views, inspired by the sincere, fresh outlook of his pretty journalism instructor. He finally realizes in the film's naturally happy conclusion that they both have a lot to offer each other. Such an ending happens to carry a great deal of symbolic import respecting the perennial conflict in the American educational experience between learning by doing and learning by theorizing.

In *Mother Is a Freshman* (20th Century-Fox, 1949), the relationship between student and teacher is amusingly reversed when a parent (Loretta Young) and her daughter (Betty Lynn) vie for the attentions of their English professor, played by Van Johnson.[22] The handsome instructor is more attracted to the mother, for whose affections he must compete with a stuffy attorney (Rudy Vallee) whom Miss Young wants to give the brush-off. Because of the complications created by the daughter, who has spurned the advances of the campus football hero in order to concentrate on her English prof, Johnson finds out that Miss Young is not to be easily won over, and a series of problems have to be resolved before he finally does win out. Although this film still reveals the influence of the collegiate romantic comedies of the 1930s, it does make some interesting contributions to the tradition, especially in emphasizing the repercussions of the generation gap, which even then were becoming increasingly evident, and in time would inspire a more serious dramatic slant in the collegiate movie. Another fine touch in *Mother Is a Freshman* is its somewhat satirical approach to the academic institution's system of utilizing and awarding scholarship funds. Because Miss Young's great grandmother has set up a scholarship that, according to the college catalog, is to be awarded to "any female of high morals, good character and refinement, with the name of Abigail Fortitude, who

Teacher's Pet **(Paramount, 1958), Clark Gable's only collegiate picture, was an entertaining romp with Doris Day, who plays the role of a journalism instructor.**

wishes to advance her education and culture," Miss Young happens to qualify on all counts as well as possessing the same first two names. Undoubtedly, such a scholarship would have since gone begging for recipients, for other than the name itself being a handicap, the qualities that the original Abigail Fortitude established must be extremely difficult for most of today's young women to cultivate.

Still another variation on the collegiate familial theme was *Peggy* (Universal-International, 1950) in which a professor and his daughters become involved in the annual Tournament of Roses celebration in Pasadena. Charles Coburn is a retired professor whose girls, Diana Lynn and Barbara Lawrence, enter the Rose Bowl Queen contest, only to find the situation complicated by Miss Lynn's secret marriage to a Ohio State football star (Rock Hudson) whose team is to play in the game. Since only unmarried girls are eligible to win the pageant, audience interest is sharpened by the suspense of whether or not Miss Lynn's secret will be discovered. Adding to the dramatic conflict is the natural clash, so meaningfully expressed in *The Male Animal,* between the scholarly Coburn and the athletic Hudson. This situation arouses even more than the usual audience interest since the old professor is unaware that football hero Hudson is really his son-in-law. In the long run, of course, everything comes out all right for everybody, as it must in this kind of movie. The most interestingly worthwhile thing about *Peggy,* actually, was the casting of that grand old man, Charles Coburn, in one of his many collegiate roles. Coburn (1877–1961), a stage-trained actor who did not perform in film until he was in his forties, seemed best in a part that called for a personality with a tough exterior but a warm and sensitive inner side. Whether cast as an administrator, a professor, or a coach, he somehow always managed to project this demeanor.

That football coaches have family problems like anyone else was the inspiration for the plot of the 1949 comedy, *Father Was a Fullback* (20th Century-Fox), in which Fred MacMurray is a coach who has to tolerate not only the misfortunes of his losing football team but also the boy-chasing antics of his daughter (Betty Lynn) whom he hopes will settle down if he can match her off with the right fellow. Even his maid (Thelma Ritter) is a thorn in his side as she continually berates MacMurray's team for losing, even going so far as to bet against it to make some quick money. Only Maureen O'Hara, in the role of the long-suffering coach's spouse, offers him a sense of stability and the moral support he so desperately needs. Although the big game with Tulane University is lost, both MacMurray's team and his domestic life appear headed for a brighter day when his daughter's latest beau, a highly sought-after grid star, spurns a grant-in-aid to Notre Dame to enroll in MacMurray's school. Through its comic perspective on the off-field concerns of the football coach, *Father*

This ad for *Father Was a Fullback* (20th Century-Fox, 1949) reveals a popular movie trend of the late 1940s and previews the dramatic form that television would refer to as the "situation comedy."

Was a Fullback takes a revered image down from its pedestal to humanize it in what could be looked upon as another preview of the television situation comedies of the 1950s.

However, some films of this era started to look back, and in two Paramount comedies of the 1940s we can detect a nostalgic mood beginning to manifest itself in the collegiate movie tradition. *Those Were the Days* (1940) saw William Holden romancing Bonita Granville and Ezra Stone lending comic support in a rather colorless film of college days in the earlier part of this century—that period when many of the social traditions of student college life are supposed to have been established.[23] A more successful attempt at conveying a nostalgic period atmosphere was *Our Hearts Were Growing Up* (Paramount, 1946), the sequel to the popularly received *Our Hearts Were Young and Gay* (1944), based on the best-selling books by the team of Cornelia Otis Skinner and Emily Kimbrough.[24] The second film continued the original's attempt to recapture the look and feel of the 1920s as Gail Russell and Diana Lynn defy the strict rules of their girls' school to steal away with their boy friends for a party weekend that includes the Harvard-Princeton football game. To obtain permission from the school administration, the girls invent an "Uncle Eddie" to act as their chaperone. But when the boy friend who is to play the role can't make it to the train station to meet them, Gail and Diana talk a bootlegger (Brian Donlevy) into playing the part. Actually, he sees in the unwitting girls a way to smuggle two suitcases of booze past the watchful eyes of the police at the station. Because of the constraints of Prohibition, there follows a series of complications that create some strained moments for the principals but plenty of laughs for the audience. True to the expectations for this kind of movie, everything works out fine in the end. The most interesting thing about watching a film like this today is that it affords us a refreshing contrast between the behavior and attitudes of an infinitely more innocent time and the questioning and polarized posture of recent years. Perhaps some day, even the social excesses and pressing personal problems of the present will generate their own special brand of nostalgia—a trend already developing, we note, in the expanding interest in the turbulent decade of the 1960s, and one which we will discuss in more detail in the final section of this book.

For much the same reason that series features would prove to be so popular on television beginning in the 1950s, this kind of fare was a favorite of moviegoers during the 1940s, particularly those who frequented the neighborhood theaters where the popular B series were mostly shown. To keep up with the demand for this kind of entertainment, a variety of familiar faces from popular series found themselves performing in a collegiate setting at one time or another. The precedent for this type of the college-life movie was set during the second half of the 1920s with the appearance of a Universal series of shorts called *The Collegians,* whose popularity was no doubt inspired by the period's fascination with the social side of the collegiate experience. Playing opposite a young lady named Dorothy Gulliver, George Lewis was the star of these shorts whose sketchy plots were mostly concerned with his involvement in extracurricular activities. Colored by the usual dormitory capers, fraternity social events, athletic contests, dating problems, and class competitions, the shorts drew most of their dramatic flavor from good-guy Lewis's confrontations with the conventional bully or cad of juvenile school-life fiction. The series was unique, however, in that its central character was carried from his freshman year at Calford right on to graduation during the four-year span of 1926 to 1929. To audiences it didn't really matter if George Lewis hardly ever found time to make it to class, for he was an appealing, personable kind of fellow, the epitome of the American college boy to whom moviegoers would readily grant an *A* in sociability if nothing else.[25]

The fiction of George Fitch was the inspiration for *Those Were the Days* (Paramount, 1940). Hazing by upperclassmen played a big part in this film about college life in the earlier part of this century. That's William Holden curtsying to the left of Ezra Stone.

The George Lewis of the 1940s was Mickey Rooney, who performed spiritedly and dynamically as the eternal juvenile, Andy Hardy. This extremely popular series was built around themes and subject matter that had a wide family appeal, and three of the films dealt both indirectly and directly with the collegiate experience. In *Andy Hardy's Double Life* (MGM, 1942), Andy is preparing to attend Wainwright College, the staid old alma mater of his father, Judge Hardy. Much to the annoyance of Andy, the judge insists that he get off on the right foot at school. But the judge (Lewis Stone) and his interfering ways are only part of Andy's problems in preparing for college. In making a play for the attractive house guest of his girl friend Polly (Ann Rutherford), Andy soon learns a lot about the unfathomable ways of women. It seems that Polly's friend (Esther Williams, in her first movie role) is a psychology student at college who knows enough about her subject matter to teach Andy a real lesson about what it means to play around with the girls. However, the most

unusual twist to this movie has Andy, in his usual man-to-man talk
with the judge, giving out advice rather than receiving it. In fact,
Andy makes it clear that if his father wants Andy to be a college man,
then it's high time he allows Andy enough independence to act like
one. In each of the films in this series there was always a lesson
intended in these talks, and college-age youth of the day must have
greatly appreciated the intent of this one.

   With the appearance of *Andy Hardy's Blonde Trouble* (1944), Andy
has finally made it to college, where he finds his women problems
compounded by his relationship with two attractive blonde co-eds
who happen to be twins (Lee and Lyn Wilde). Beginning with the
opening train sequence in which Andy sets off for college, something
of Harold Lloyd's role in *The Freshman* shines through when Andy
becomes involved in a series of social entanglements largely of his
own doing. Eager to prove his independence as a college man, Andy
discovers that adaptation to college life is not an easy thing, especially when he meets a new girl friend (Bonita Granville) whom he
tries to romance while he becomes involved in the affairs of the
appealing twins. By the close of the picture, Andy somehow manages
to resolve his problems, assert his approaching manhood, and win the

**One of Mickey Rooney's social problems at college came in the attractive shape of twins
Lyn and Lee Wilde in *Andy Hardy's Blonde Trouble* (MGM, 1944).**

approval of his dad. The Andy Hardy series, which among other things, extolled the American quality of self-reliance through its various characterizations, interpreted college as a place where one must learn to face up to personal problems and to adjust socially to those experiences which the college-life movie has always intimated are more important than what happens in the classroom.[26]

If a film series stayed around long enough, it invariably found its way into the collegiate scene.[27] The same observation applies to popular screen comics and comedy teams, for their performing in college-life films has been a long and honorable tradition. Thus it was only a matter of time before the most popular comedy team of the 1940s got around to making its contribution to the tradition. The team, of course, was Bud Abbott and Lou Costello, and the movie was *Here Come the Co-eds* (Universal, 1945). Like so many of their films, this one contains a number of musical interludes, and befitting a story that takes place on the campus of a woman's college, features Phil Spitalny's all-girl orchestra of the then popular radio program, "The Hour of Charm," in one of the movie's finest production numbers. It is the energetic Peggy Ryan, though, who comes through as the real scene-stealer of this picture in her song-and-dance routines.

With a movie popularity that began in the early 1940s, Bud Abbott and Lou Costello had become fairly predictable by this time in their careers. As caretakers at Miss Ryan's school, the boys become involved in helping the students raise enough money to write off the school's mortgage debt, which (absurdly enough) happens to be held by the chairman of the governing board—an individual who obviously does not have the best interests of the school at heart. Typically, the film's dramatic contrast of educational types is presented through the roles of the board chairman (Charles Dingle), who certainly looks the part of a skinflint, and the progressive but beleaguered college dean (Donald Cook), who would like to rid his college of its stultifying traditions. To raise sufficient funds to pay off the mortgage, the students schedule a concert by Spitalny's all-girl orchestra; a wrestling match in which fall-guy Costello takes on a masked foe (Lon Chaney, Jr.); and a basketball game in which Lou, as a team member, performs in drag and provides the laugh highlight of the movie. As it does for all movie comedians, the collegiate background really functions in *Here Come the Co-eds* as a vehicle to project the principals' special brand of humor—in this case, Abbott and Costello's slapstick inheritance from burlesque.

A much more interesting and human situation was that involving the most popular comedy team of the 1950s—Dean Martin and Jerry Lewis—in *That's My Boy* (Paramount, 1951). Even though this picture reveals overtones of just about every college-life film made up to its time, it somehow manages to come across with a degree of originality, mainly because it tries to sympathize with the actual feelings of a negative personality. Jerry Lewis is the son of "Jarring Jack" Jackson (Eddie Mayehoff), a former all-American football star at Ridgeville University. When Jack Senior discovers to his disappointment and disgrace that his anemic son has no desire to play football, he recruits star player Bill Baker (Dean Martin) for his alma mater with the understanding that the Ridgeville coach will allow Junior to make the team. However, Junior turns out to be such a poor player that in the opening game he even scores a touchdown for the opposing team. After his roommate Bill coaches him in secret and shows him how to stand on his own feet and ignore his father's dominance, Junior goes on to become the star of the big game, and the movie ends on a happy note. Ruth Hussey is impressive as Junior's understanding mother while Polly Bergen makes an attractive co-ed, but the real reason for this movie's success is Eddie Mayehoff's performance as the self-centered ex-jock whose only aim in middle-life, it seems, is to relive his former athletic glory through his son's experiences. In its depiction of the strained relationship between two individuals alienated through lack of understanding and communication, *That's My Boy* exhibits the movies' growing emphasis at this time on psychological insight into characterization. In its dramatic conflict between father and son this comedy contained the essential ingredients for a serious film study.

By the 1950s, a standard of living and a popular base had been achieved which saw American youth flocking to college campuses in wholesale numbers. Still, for many families, the attendance of a son or daughter at college was a milestone in that such an event represented the first time a member of their clan had ever attended college. For the parents, there was a kind of magic in such an accomplishment, which we see reflected in films like *Saturday's Hero* (1951) and *Take Care of My Little Girl* (20th Century-Fox 1951). Both leading roles in these exemplary films reflect the tenor of the times conditioned by the organizational attitude of business and industry in that they depict individuals as being subjected to the pervasive power of a system and without too much to say about their own situations. The fact that this was the first generation to be exposed to the dominant visual control of television reveals a degree of insight into its characteristic mood of submissiveness. Without much questioning their lot or roles in life, the college students of the 1950s, in the first wave of the democratizing effects and economic upswing during the years following World War II, apparently felt that they were very fortunate to be attending college in the first place. When in awe of a strange and wondrous new environment, one speaks in hushed tones—if at all.

By the 1950s, too, it had become clear to moviegoers that the collegiate experience was not so elite after all; anyone with the proper motivation could go to college. There was no guarantee of the results, of course, but the inevitable democratization of the college experience had now become more pronounced in our society, and the movies did not hesitate to reflect this change. Evidence for this kind of outlook began to appear as early as 1942 in a movie called *Harvard, Here I Come* (Columbia), which starred the rugged ex-boxer "Slapsie" Maxie Rosenbloom. As the owner of a popular night club, Maxie gets the Harvard Lampoon award for stupidity—a dubious honor, of course, but one that inspires him to enroll in the college. With his reputation for mangling the English language, the former heavyweight fighter sparks a great deal of excitement among the professors of the anthropology department, who theorize that in Maxie they might have discovered the missing link with primitive man. Despite this amusing situation, though, the movie proceeds to overlook a ripe opportunity to satirize the educational establishment, and in the process falls flat on its face. The circumstance of the redoubtable Maxie leading the life of an average student—attending classes, joining a fraternity, and even making it through a term at a formidable institution like Harvard—should have provided sufficient grist for an above-average college-life comedy with a decided satirical slant, but somehow the disjointed script goes out of its way to avoid the appealing subtleties of this angle. Even so, there are some fine humorous moments, especially those concerning the professors who see Maxie as the key to understanding the evolutionary process.

Ten years later even the Bowery Boys, those refugees from the wrong side of the tracks, made it to college in *Hold That Line* (Monogram, 1952), another of the numerous films in this long-running series. Typically, the thin plot is nothing more than a series of pegs on which the boys, dominated as usual by Leo Gorcey and Huntz Hall, can hang their gags and slapstick routines, which here turn on the futile attempts to introduce them to the finer aspects of higher education. However, the collegiate background allows the boys to romp through a wide range of their usual mindless escapades, climaxing with the inevitable big football game and the boys' special version of the old college try. Veda Ann Borg, whose movie career began in the 1930s, was still around to add to the feminine interest. Both Gorcey and Hall had begun their typed careers in the 1930s, too, as members of the original Dead End Kids.

While they failed to make the most of Slapsie Maxie Rosenbloom and the Bowery Boys at college, though, the movies seemed to have better luck with animals. Such comic situations have to be the ultimate takeoff on the college-life caper, particularly the films that featured a chimpanzee named Bonzo. In the initial movie, *Bedtime for Bonzo* (Universal-International, 1951), Ronald Reagan is a psychology professor who uses Bonzo in an experiment to prove that environment, not heredity, is what determines a child's behavior pattern. Naturally, this situation affords the script a ripe opportunity to lampoon the collegiate film's favorite academic targets—the field of psychology and its obsessive attempts to categorize and simplify the complexities of human behavior. When Bonzo steals a necklace from a jewelry store, Professor Reagan's theories are put to the test, as they are whenever any movie educator goes against the grain of the system to prove his stand. To complicate matters further, Reagan's dramatic antagonist happens to be the college dean to whose daughter he is engaged. Jealous of the girl (Diana Lynn) whom Reagan has hired to tend Bonzo, the dean's daughter breaks off her engagement with him. When Reagan is accused of the jewelry theft, things look dark for him until Miss Lynn saves the day by bringing forth evidence that Bonzo is the culprit. Professor Reagan's environmental theories may have been shot full of holes, but the movie's ending implies that he will soon take an important step toward improving his own environment by marrying Miss Lynn.

For one reason or another—perhaps due to the popular success of the True Life Adventure series of the Walt Disney studios—movies

In what could be the ultimate takeoff on the college-life movie tradition, *Bonzo Goes to College* **(Universal-International, 1952), an affable chimp named Bonzo becomes the quarterback for his football team. Here, he is pictured with his coach Edmund Gwenn (left), Gene Lockhart, and Gigi Perreau.**

that featured animals either in real life or in fantasy, were extremely popular in the 1950s.[28] The audience appeal of Bonzo's acting talent brought forth a sequel in 1952, though with a different cast and a new role for Bonzo. The improbable but crowd-pleasing plot of *Bonzo Goes to College* (Universal-International) finds Bonzo taking a college entrance examination after a loser of a coach (Edmund Gwenn) discovers that Bonzo can handle a football better than any of his regular players. In fact, the chimp is particularly adept at throwing the ball with distance and accuracy, so good, in fact, that Bonzo becomes the star quarterback of his school's team and leads it to victory in the big game. No doubt many a real-life player of the day took a lot of ribbing when this film came out. A plot situation that would allow a chimp to become a college student, let alone a superior athlete, is a telling comment on the attitudes of both Hollywood and the public toward the democratization of the collegiate experience during the 1950s.

By this time, movies of a more serious bent had also begun to interpret our colleges and universities as national agents of the democratic process, and the increasing numbers of nontraditional students did much to sensitize the movie people to this new vision of the college-life experience. One of the better satirical take-offs in this light was *Mr. Belvedere Goes to College* (20th Century-Fox, 1949) with Clifton Webb in the role of the pompous, acid-tongued, and self-assured character he had created in *Sitting Pretty* (1947).[29] This time around, Mr. Belvedere enrolls in college with the idea of completing a four-year program in one year—a task he is highly confident he can carry out, much to the amazement and shocked disbelief of his professors. Procuring a job as a waiter in a sorority house to help defray his expenses, Mr. Belvedere proceeds to breeze through his academic program while also finding time to help out with his associates' problems. Shirley Temple's part as a war-widowed student with a child provides this film's unique romantic interest when a student (Tom Drake) falls in love with her, a situation which not only reveals Belvedere's penchant for analyzing human nature but also belies his crusty exterior. He thus accomplishes his educational goal and becomes a favorite among the students. Mr. Belvedere's experience as a microcosm of the quickly changing scene of the college campus in the late 1940s was only a small sample of what lay ahead, and his peculiar attitude toward the educational establishment and process was prophetic of the future questioning of the traditional approach to earning a college degree. Such an outlook, which questioned the lockstep patterns of degree programs, not only provided the basis for the film's satirical comment, it supplied a certain amount of insight into what might be wrong with the conventional educational process itself.

Clifton Webb's cynicism and Shirley Temple's idealism combine for an instructively entertaining comedy—*Mr. Belvedere Goes to College* (20th Century-Fox, 1949).

Apartment for Peggy (20th Century-Fox, 1948), another film structured around a different approach to the educational experience, attempted to dramatize what it was like for a young married couple to hack it out while the husband was a G.I. Bill student. The couple, portrayed by Jeanne Crain and William Holden, are compelled to make the necessary sacrifices while he seeks his ultimate goal of a college degree. Soon Holden begins to question whether or not he should continue to deprive his dedicated wife of the finer things of life, while Miss Crain, in retaining her enthusiasm and idealism throughout any problem that arises, inspires him to continue with his course of studies.

It was a common enough experience during this time, of course, as college campuses became overcrowded with married students after the war, but a unique dimension to this film is the role of Edmund Gwenn as a retired philosophy professor who is down on everything and contemplating suicide. Because of the housing shortage created by the large student influx, the old professor shares his quarters with the young people, and in their dogged persistence to prepare for a better life he recognizes a positive human quality that awakens in him his dormant love for life.

Having won an Academy Award in 1947 for his role in *Miracle on 34th Street,* Gwenn turned in another inspired performance in this later film. Edmund Gwenn endeared himself to moviegoers as an accomplished character actor from the time he arrived in Hollywood from England in the 1930s, but his role in *Apartment for Peggy* was unique both for him and for the collegiate film tradition in that it revealed a facet of the professorial type that had by and large been overlooked in previous films—that dark side of the human condition usually reserved for tragic characters. The movies' fascination with this side of the man of learning became more pronounced in this period and continued into the 1960s and 1970s, as we shall see.[30]

The *film noir* trend of the 1940s was represented in the collegiate film tradition by *The Accused* (Paramount, 1949), a taut drama in which Loretta Young appears as a psychology professor who kills a student bent on raping her. Although she pleads self-defense, Miss Young is moved to make the killing look like an accident to avoid the notoriety attendant to a murder trial. Obviously, Hollywood still felt that the college teacher, especially a woman, had an air of respectability to uphold. The ensuing sequence of events sets up an intriguing courtroom drama between the defense (Robert Cummings) and the prosecution (Wendell Corey), and results in a showdown between Corey and Miss Young, both of whom take equal acting honors in this picture. In a movie like *The Accused,* Hollywood not only began to deal with socially questionable and relatively taboo subject matter, it put this new subject matter in a realistic perspective by revealing that even a respectable member of society could be involved in such goings-on.

Concurrently, a more graphic attention to students' extracurricular activities other than just social events and football games began to express itself.[31] The elite system of college fraternities and sororities had begun to be questioned as early as 1939's *Sorority House* but by 1944 the social defects of the sorority setting had become familiar enough for it to be utilized as a unique background for an entertaining murder mystery called *Nine Girls* (Columbia). Featuring Evelyn Keyes, Jinx Falkenburg, Anita Louise, and Nina Foch as four of the sorority sisters and Ann Harding as their chaperone, this picture transferred the scene of primary action from the campus to a mountain lodge owned by the chapter. Ironically, the change of scene is dramatically effective because it affords us a better opportunity to look at the principals as individuals, since thy are now divorced from the familiar social surroundings of their college. (In their talk and behavior, though, these girls come across to audiences as bona fide products of their time's collegiate environment.) The fact that all the other members disliked the slain girl (Anita Louise) adds to the complications of solving the murder and points out the clannish ways that can hinder any attempt at communication in an organization like this. With the girls coming across as distinct personalities, however, it isn't long before an audience can put all the clues together and determine who the culprit is. Because this movie was made during the heart of the war years when male actors were scarce, one reviewer made an amusing, but perceptive, observation that more problems are solved in *Nine Girls* than just that of a murder: "One is what to do to dodge the male actor shortage. Simply use gals and have them refer to their men in conversation. . . ."[32] Perhaps this was the primary reason for that lonely mountain setting.

In 1951, a serious attempt at criticizing the sorority system was produced in an embarrassingly naïve film called *Take Care of My Little Girl* (20th Century-Fox). The more successful production, *Saturday's Hero,* which attacked the abuses of big-time college football, appeared in the same year, suggesting that the public was now receptive to a more critical look at our system of higher education. Although the intent of *Take Care of My Little Girl* was to satirize the snobbish and callous ways of a social organization dedicated to perpetuating antidemocratic manners, the picture simply did not move audiences that by this time were better informed about the collegiate experience. The tenuous plot was another reason for this movie's failure to get its message across. In the story, Jeanne Crain finds out about sororities the hard way as a wide-eyed freshman who through her acquaintance with popular Mitzi Gaynor is accepted into membership while her closest friend is turned down and quits school in disgrace. Jeanne meets Dale Robertson, who is antifraternity, but she spurns him when she becomes attracted to college man Jeffrey Hunter. Finally she realizes that Hunter is nothing but a spoiled snob and breaks up with him, but it takes a near tragedy during Hell Week for Jeanne to decide that sororities are not for her and that Dale

Take Care of My Little Girl (20th Century-Fox, 1951), supposedly an exposé of the sorority system, saw big-man-on-campus Jeffrey Hunter and sorority pledge Jeanne Crain socializing at the campus malt shop.

Robertson is. Although the film projects some highly charged dramatic moments, it fails to properly follow up on them, and as a result does not pack the solid punch that this kind of movie should.[33] It would be twenty-six years before a really superior film (*Fraternity Row,* Paramount, 1977) would present the most realistic interpretation of the collegiate social club that had ever appeared in the college-life movie tradition (see chapter 4).

Playing to mixed reviews, *Goodbye, My Fancy* (Warner Brothers, 1951) was a film whose content and thematic approach pointed to the kinds of collegiate movies that would appear more frequently in the 1960s and 1970s. Because of its concentration on the involvement of individuals within a social system, this production comes across as an even mixture of both comic and dramatic action—as most latently serious collegiate movies have always done.

Joan Crawford is Agatha Reed, a progressive, modish congresswoman who has been invited back to her alma mater to receive an honorary degree. However, we find out that Crawford was expelled from the college some twenty years before for having spent a night away from campus, thus breaking one of the strictest rules of this renowned private school. Later, we also discover that she had been out that night with her history professor (Robert Young), who has since risen through the ranks to become president of the college. In renewing this old romance, Miss Crawford receives a proposal of marriage from Young, but things begin to happen that cause her to revise her opinion of him. When she is denied the chance to show the students a film that, ironically, deals with the state control of education in totalitarian countries, she realizes for the first time that President Young is only a pawn of the board of trustees. However, she counters their decision that the film's content is unsuitable for the students with a threat to reveal what really happened between her and Young twenty years ago. The film is then scheduled, and Miss Crawford not only receives her honorary degree, she decides that the real romance in her life is her long-time associate Frank Lovejoy, a *Life* magazine photographer assigned to do the pictures for her honorary degree story.

In spite of its pervasive atmosphere of comedy, *Goodbye, My Fancy* carries on the serious tradition of the collegiate movie whose dramatic conflict grows out of the rebellious relationship of the individual to the system. A subplot underscoring the controversy surrounding congresswoman Reed's efforts to show her film to the students deals with the suppression of academic freedom when one of the college's most popular professors is put on the spot because of his crusade against social ignorance and indifference. In the early 1950s, the theme of *The Male Animal* was obviously still alive and timely.

But there was another 1950s film about another kind of system, the military academy, that left a vivid impression on those who saw it and pointed directly toward the predominant mood of the college movies of the 1960s. *The Strange One* (Columbia, 1957) was based on Calder Willingham's novel *End as a Man*. Ben Gazzara is Jocko DeParis, a cadet at a southern military college who exercises a satanic hold over his classmates. Out to buck a system that apparently would deny him his self-identity, DeParis uses his gullible classmates to carry out his designs for revenge on the school's executive officer for having disciplined him in front of the entire cadet corps. When his motives are found out, DeParis is pronounced guilty by a kangaroo court and is sentenced to be railroaded out of the academy. With its psychological slant and insight into abberant behavior, *The Strange One* provides an original twist on the theme of the individual and his response to the demands of a societal setting, and exists as one of the first collegiate films to strike a grim note of realism concerning this theme. The days of *Flirtation Walk* and *Brother Rat* were gone forever, and the movies were on the verge of creating a series of shock waves through a radically different approach to interpreting social behavior and experience.

Ben Gazzara's antimilitary behavior provokes the reprimand of the academy's commandant (Clifton James) in *The Strange One* **(Columbia, 1957).**

As if *The Strange One* were not harbinger enough of things to come, Hollywood even came up with its college-life version of the horror film in 1958—*Monster on the Campus* (Universal-International).[34] Conventional enough by horror film standards, this is the story of a college professor (Arthur Franz) who becomes a victim of biological regression when he comes in contact with the blood of a fish still in its original state of evolution. This predicament has the tragic result of transforming the professor back into a primitive form

who rampages the campus as a murdering beast. In a strangely ironic
sense, this movie was an unwitting portent and symbol of the stigma
that many students would come to attach to their college and university leaders during the troubled and turbulent times of the late 1960s.
It also struck a mood that would carry over into the early 1970s.

4 Reactions, Rebellions, and Reminiscences: The 1960s–1970s

I'm not satisfied with Yale as a magnificent factory on democratic business lines; I dream of something else, something visionary, a great institution not of boys, clean, lovable and honest, but of men of brains, of courage, of leadership, a great center of thought, to stir the country and bring it back to the understanding of what man creates with his imagination, and dares with his will. It's visionary—it will come.

> —character in
> Owen Johnson's
> *Stover at Yale* (1912)

In a world where "service" is universally demanded, the universities alone are licensed to subvert; though naturally the language in which this patent is expressed is far from frank or even lucid. To "free the mind" or "liberate the spirit," these are the conventional names for the kind of education, the dangerous enterprise to which our colleges are pledged.

> —Leslie A. Fiedler,
> "The Crumbling Ivory Tower" (1964)

Steve Allen, that genial, highly talented, and professorial-looking television personality, never really made it big in the movies and probably never has even cared to, although he has performed creditably in a number of screen roles. Ironically, though, in a 1960 B movie that exploited the increasingly liberal attitudes toward social behavior at that time, he gave what many movie fans think was his finest performance. Tantalizingly titled *College Confidential* (Universal-International), the movie purported to tell the story of a dedicated sociology professor who, upon conducting a sex-habits survey among his students, is brought to trial in the small college town where he teaches. Allen plays his part with sincerity and conviction, and in the high point of the film—his courtroom speech after being acquitted— demonstrates that he could respond movingly to the demands of the dramatic moment. In his contribution to the film tradition of the crusading academic type, Allen observes that the true intent of his unpopular survey was to lead people out of ignorance in order to help them better understand themselves, implying that such an honorable quest is always at the heart of the educational process even though at times this motive may be greatly out of tune with the will and interests of the general populace. Allen's handling of the issue of academic freedom was, of course, reminiscent of *The Male Animal* and *Goodbye, My Fancy,* but this film's frank approach to the controversial subject of sex was something different, a preview of the 1960s as an era that would uncover subject matter viewers thought could never be shown on the screen of a public theater. In truth, the overall tone and manner of the collegiate film during the 1960s appears to be suffused with sexual fascination and social intrigue, mainly because by this time the censorship barriers had been broken by a more liberal popular attitude toward subjects that traditionally had been taboo. It was an atmosphere that had been developing since the 1950s, but with the 1960s came a social permissiveness that brought with it a flood of films mirroring society's newfound freedom to express itself.

That the collegiate movie could exploit sex in a highly sensational manner was revealed in a 1964 murder melodrama called *Psychomania* (Victoria), which featured the dubious added attraction of sadism. The plot revolves around two brutal co-ed murders at a women's college and the eventual tracking down of the culprit, who in the best tradition of the murder mystery movie turns out to be the least likely suspect in the cast. Of this lackluster group, Shepperd Strudwick, in the role of a suave, confident attorney, turns in the most notable performance. As a variation of the collegiate murder mystery film tradition dating from *College Scandal* in the 1930s, *Psychomania* reflects both the growing interest in psychological themes and deviant behavior and the open-ended approach to what one reviewer termed "the sexploitation market" since "it frequently borders on the pornographic."[1]

In a much lighter vein, the sex symbol of *College Confidential,* Mamie Van Doren, appeared in another movie that unwittingly pointed out the increasingly dominant role of advancing technology and computerized systems in higher education: *Sex Kittens Go to College* (Allied Artists, 1960). Miss Van Doren plays Dr. Mathilda

A sexy co-ed perched on the desk of professor Steve Allen helped sell *College Confidential* (Universal-International, 1960) to the moviegoing public during the 1960s—a time when the sensational side of social experience began to draw attention.

West, who ostensibly possesses a brain to match her curves, having amassed thirteen degrees and a knowledge of eighteen languages. Because of these apparent qualifications, she is chosen, sight unseen, by a computer called THINKO to head the science department at Collins College. Upon her arrival, however, Miss Van Doren's physical attributes arouse both the jealous envy of the women faculty and the amorous fascination of the men, all of whom had expected a spinster type to fill the position. The star football player (Woo Woo Grabowski) is especially taken by her presence, and he expresses his feelings by fainting dead away at the very sight of her.

Because Dr. Zorch (Louis Nye), the computer's director, has programmed it to pick racehorse winners, a mob boss is prompted to send two of his hit men to put the finger on one "Sam Thinko," an uncannily lucky bettor who has cost the mobster a great deal of money. Although Miss Van Doren's real past as a nightclub performer is revealed by the gunmen (her stage name: the Tallahassee Tassel Tosser), she accepts the marriage offer of the college's benefactor (Jackie Coogan), a Texas millionaire playboy. This situation and the curing of THINKO's propensity to gamble brings about a happy resolution to a surprisingly entertaining story. *Sex Kittens Go to College* was obviously influenced by several past collegiate films: in particular, the gangster element of *Rise and Shine* and Virginia Mayo's disguised showgirl role in *She's Working Her Way through College*. But other than the satirical take-off on the computer's growing influence, this film's most original feature was its casual attitude toward exhibiting the female body, specifically in the persons of Miss Van Doren, Tuesday Weld, and Mijanou Bardot. In fulfilling the promise of its title, *Sex Kittens Go to College* displays an abundant array of bosoms and bottoms with a detached perspective that today would be labeled "sexist" in its intent. Also reflective of the period's increasingly liberal outlook was the casting of two gay professor roles, one played by long-time character actor John Carradine.

The sensitive subject of homosexuality, particularly in the collegiate film, has had a tough time in breaking through the barriers of censorship, but the 1960s saw a distinct loosening of the restrictions governing this kind of behavior. In 1936, Lillian Hellman's play *The Children's Hour* (which centered around lesbianism at a young girls' private school) was made into a rather harmless film *(These Three);* it was remade in 1962 with its original title and obviously with its original dramatic intent. By the time of *Sex Kittens,* though, its gay professor roles come across as socially acceptable mainly because they are presented within the overall context of comedy, whose conventions readily permit distorted social behavior. Not until the 1970s is reference to homosexuality in the serious collegiate movie allowed more obvious overtones, for example, the role of the British professor in *Butley* (American Film Theater, 1974).[2]

Another thematic but controversial subject of expanding interest at this time was the conflict between generations, which would take on its most serious manifestations toward the end of the 1960s. A prime example of the college film's rather innocent approach to the clash of youth and age in the early part of the decade was *Take Her, She's Mine* (20th Century-Fox, 1963) in which James Stewart packs his seemingly sheltered daughter (Sandra Dee) off to college, and eventually discovers to his dismay that the experience has drastically transformed the innocent adolescent he once knew. Affecting a sophisticated posture and zealous identification with the expanding social causes and controversies of the time, Miss Dee proceeds to bewilder her father at every turn, and Stewart turns in another of his average-man-mystified-by-it-all roles which delighted movie audiences so much. Based on a Broadway play, the movie's plot is compellingly entertaining, highlighted by the acting of Stewart, Audrey Meadows as his practical-minded and understanding wife, and Robert Morley as a world-weary Britisher. On a serious note, Stewart's puzzled outlook concerning the social vagaries and outrageous behavior of his rebellious daughter must have characterized the atmosphere of many a household throughout the country at that time. It was a mood that would keep proliferating and eventually explode in the campus uprisings of the late 1960s.

But the tenor of social behavior during the earlier part of the decade was relatively calm, and another Sandra Dee collegiate film that typified this serenity was *Tammy Tell Me True* (Universal-International, 1961). As we have observed, the lead character of a popular film series almost always made it to college, provided the series lasted long enough. Such was the fate of the "Tammy" movies, which had begun in 1957 with Debbie Reynolds in the title role. In the 1961 film, Sandra Dee performs as the supposedly unspoiled country girl whose personality establishes the plot for yet another collegiate variation on the theme of the innocent rustic exposed to the sophisticated ways of the college system. As a kind of female Huckleberry Finn (she comes to college via the river and her shantyboat!), Tammy is bound to clash with the establishment and promptly proceeds to do so by falling for a professor (John Gavin). But in accordance with the standard formula for this kind of situation, it is Tammy with her natural manner who wins out in the end by teaching organized society a thing or two about human relationships. Appropriate to the atmosphere of this kind of movie, the musical score is in the syrupy, romanticized orchestral style of Percy Faith. But at this time a different, and revolutionary, style of music was beginning to make a tremendous social impact on the sensibilities of our nation's youth.

The movie musicals of the 1960s, in responding to the popular youth fads and liberated life-styles that were generated by the electronic-sound revolution, were really throwbacks to the films of the 1930s whose threadbare plots seemingly manufactured any excuse to present a musical number. But while most youth-slanted musicals of the 1930s could appeal to a more general audience whose tastes were not as sophisticated as those of later moviegoers, vehicles of the 1960s seemed to be exclusively directed at high-school and college-age students who had begun to cultivate interests that reflected their free-and-easy codes of behavior. The fact that movies were consciously being produced for a special age group at this time also pointed out the ever widening gap between the cultural interests and social values of the older and younger generations. For example, *For Those Who Think Young* (United Artists, 1964), whose title was inspired by a popular soft drink's advertising pitch, concentrates on youth's susceptibility to faddish status symbols by romanticizing what was then referred to as a "cool" life-style. The setting is an oceanside college where, in the direct tradition of the 1930s collegiate musical, no one ever seems to go to class. Instead, the entire student body spends its time beaching, surfing, and crowding into a nightclub to watch performers like James Darren and Nancy Sinatra sing and comics Woody Woodbury and Paul Lynde go through their routines. We even find the teachers getting into the action, apparently because they don't have any classes to teach. Ellen McRae stands out as a sociology professor who chucks her formal ways to hobnob with the students and their wild social scene. In Miss McRae's performance the 1930s' concept of the popular prof as one who is in tune with the latest goings-on was apparently still alive.[3]

The stock situation of the hayseed character come to the big campus shows up again in *C'mon Let's Live a Little* (Paramount, 1967), when pop singer Bobby Vee plays a farm boy whose natural manner overcomes the confusing events of the late-1960s campus scene. The farm boy is exploited by a student protester in his free-speech movement—another sign of what lay just around the corner. Vee adapts to this role in a way that proves he could act creditably as well as sing. With the casting of playboy baseball pitcher Bo Belinsky as the proprietor of the night spot where all the action takes place, Hollywood maintained its convention of capitalizing on an athlete's name. In general, though, this period in the history of the collegiate movie was a time when the genre's conventions and the revolutionary attitudes in the wind began to commingle and suggest a radically different approach to dramatizing social behavior and relationships.

An example of this subtle transition lay in the fact that during the 1960s the traditional sports-oriented movie all but disappeared, and when it did resurface, it was mainly for satirical purposes. Undoubtedly, the widespread popularity of professional sports (particularly football, which recruited its players from the college ranks) had a great deal to do with changing public attitudes, and Hollywood's reaction to them, during this time. Even though it does not meet my definition of the collegiate film, *John Goldfarb, Please Come Home* (20th Century-Fox, 1964), through its attempt to exploit the established name of Notre Dame football, was a prime example of the changing attitudes toward some of the most hallowed images of the collegiate tradition. With a plot derived from the controversial U-2 spying incidents over the Soviet Union, this movie centers around a U-2 pilot (Richard Crenna) who makes an unscheduled landing in an oil-rich Arab country. Peter Ustinov plays the country's demented king whose son has been cut from the Notre Dame football squad. Ustinov assigns Crenna the seemingly impossible task of training a pickup team to play the Fighting Irish in an actual game. When the game does come off, the outcome is as absurd as might be expected, with feminine lead Shirley MacLaine scoring the touchdown that beats Notre Dame and locating a new oil well in the process. Considering the immense wealth of the oil-producing countries and subsequent economic and political developments, the idea behind its plot does not appear too farfetched after all.[4] The real significance of *John*

The picture that introduced Jane Fonda to the world was a film about college basketball called *Tall Story* (Warner Bros., 1960). Here, she strolls with her seemingly reluctant co-star, Tony Perkins.

Goldfarb, Please Come Home is its fearless reliance on actual events to satirize this country's bumbling manner of handling international relations—a situation that would become even more critical, as the years have revealed.

In 1960, two romantic comedies with collegiate settings appeared, both of which exemplify why this favorite form of the 1930s college-life film was now dying out. In an attempted satirical, but poorly conceived, approach to college sports, *Tall Story* (Warner Brothers) introduces Jane Fonda in her first screen role, playing the rather innocuous part of a college student in love with basketball player Tony Perkins. In view of her later acting achievements, this film was an inauspicious beginning for Miss Fonda, whose main dramatic function here appears to be little more than to contribute to the perennially perplexed look of Perkins. Passing up the opportunity to take a pointedly satirical swipe at the questionable ethics of intercollegiate athletics, the story line develops in such a way that it is difficult to determine whether Perkins's major problem is to accept a gambler's bribe to throw an upcoming game or to continue his romance with Miss Fonda. As a result, *Tall Story* unfortunately deteriorates into a mild-mannered sex farce, which was probably director Joshua Logan's underlying intent anyway.[5]

The other romantic comedy, *High Time* (20th Century-Fox), featured an aging Bing Crosby as a millionaire franchise restaurateur who enters college because he feels unfulfilled. He's now a widower, his kids are grown, and he finally has the money and time to do what he has always wanted to do: get a college education. The humor of this situation grows out of an older man's efforts to revise his dated perspective on things and adapt his set ways to a system designed primarily for the college-age group. Except for Mr. Belvedere's one-year assault on the college curriculum in 1949 (Clifton Webb in *Mr. Belvedere Goes to College*), the movies had pretty much left this kind of story alone, and even though the G.I. Bill had enabled a much older student than the norm to attend college, there had never been many middle-aged or senior-citizen students on campus, either in real life or in the movies. *High Time* was something of a first, too, in that it carried its older lead character from the freshman year through graduation, with the personable Crosby undergoing the gamut of collegiate experiences from fraternity hazing to falling in love wtih a pretty French instructor (Nicole Maurey). Although this film took considerable license with Crosby's role in order to make it fit the social pattern of what the public expected of a college student at this time, *High Time* nevertheless looked ahead to a growing influx of older students during the 1970s who would discover in the educational experience a way to expand the self and stay "alive."

With respect to the college-life movie tradition, this film can be taken as the last of the romantic comedies in the 1930s mold, carrying no hint of what lay some ten years down the road. In fact, the college president's remarks to the freshman assembly near the beginning of this movie shed a great deal of light on just how far we have come since the highly competitive experiences of students in the early 1960s: "If you don't have enough interest in your education to attend class, we have nine applicants waiting to take your place when you flunk out. And, like you, each of them also stood in the top twelve percent of his high school class. Look around you. By graduation, four years hence, the person on either side of you will no longer be with us."

Along with student competition for places in college, the 1960s and 1970s saw the college professor playing a more prominent role in the movies, not only because there were now more of them on the scene but because of the public's increased awareness of the proliferating discoveries and achievements in technology and space travel during this era. Even so, respect for the academic type in the movies was slow in coming: most brilliant professorial roles of this time come across like Ray Milland in *It Happens Every Spring* (1949), and Fred MacMurray in Walt Disney's *The Absent-Minded Professor* (Buena Vista, 1961). The latter film started a series of movies built around mythical Medfield College that lasted well into the 1970s.[6] In the Absent-Minded Professor films, wacky but wondrous inventions and formulas provide the basis for stories that appealed to the entire family; MacMurray's central role in the initial film, wherein he invents a miraculous substance ("flubber") that enables his car to fly, sets the pervasive tone for the Medfield series.

While MacMurray helped color the image of the genius professor as eccentric but harmless, certain other roles appeared to suggest a latent contempt for this type. Apparently, this negative posture was the inspiration for what many fans feel is one of Jerry Lewis's better movies—*The Nutty Professor* (Paramount, 1963). Here, Lewis is cast as a composite of the general public's stereotyped image of the college professor: introverted, uncommunicative, accident-prone, and physically unattractive. But as a chemistry professor with a laboratory in which he logs a great deal of time, Lewis comes up with a secret formula that can transform him into a suave, handsome movie-star type whom all the girls fall in love with at first sight. Actually, what we have here is an update of Joe E. Brown's role in *The Gladiator* (1938), expressed this time through the social identity needs of a college professor instead of a student. Everything seems to work smoothly for Lewis's alter ego until, at critical moments, the formula wears off and he changes back into his real self in full view of those who happen to be around. It is this untimely transformation that underscores the movie's moral: if you lack the conviction to believe in yourself, then nobody else will. Like Brown in his earlier "loser" role, Lewis also has a girl (Stella Stevens) who believes in him even though nobody else does. But it appears that in this movie the casting of a beautiful girl functions mainly to offset a negative physical type and help reiterate the American inclination to waver between illusion and reality, symbolized by the "nutty professor" whose outlook on life is contained in the clash between his fantasized ideals and

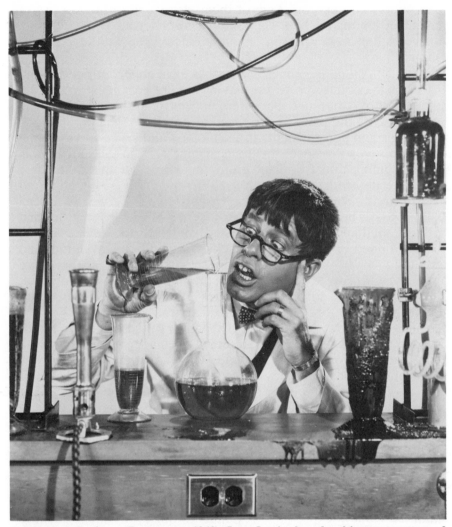

In *The Nutty Professor* (Paramount, 1963), Jerry Lewis plays the ultimate stereotype of the college professor—an ugly, bumbling chemistry teacher who invents a formula that transforms him into an irresistible glamour boy.

the realistic demands of social identity. In *The Nutty Professor,* Jerry Lewis, who directed this film and also collaborated on its script, caught something of the American preoccupation with the need for social identification and projected it significantly through the experience of a reticent type familiar to American culture.

In a pervasively comic but underlying serious vein, the college professor as loser in life as well as in the system was graphically portrayed in the film adaptation of Edward Albee's long-running

Broadway play, *Who's Afraid of Virginia Woolf?* (Warner Brothers, 1966). Married to the lustful, shrewish daughter (Elizabeth Taylor) of the college president, Richard Burton plays the role of a middle-aged history professor who has lost sight of his professional dreams and ambitions. His predicament appears on the surface to be the source of a constant barrage of humiliation and vilification from his spiteful wife during an all-night drinking party with a new faculty couple on campus (George Segal and Sandy Dennis). But as the plot develops through a series of seemingly comic episodes whose underlying implications border on the tragic, we begin to realize that it is Burton's wife who, childless and apparently lacking a sense of purpose, is the real failure in life. Her emotional outcries and accusations directed at her husband are really the pathetic attempts of a highly frustrated individual to communicate with the one person in her life she feels should understand her plight. In spite of his real-life failures, then, the professor paradoxically comes off in a more positive light because he has at least learned to live with his own failures and personal put-downs; in short, he has learned to live with himself. This distinction is at the heart of the psychological duel between the professor and his

History professor Richard Burton and his wife (Elizabeth Taylor) lead new faculty member George Segal and his wife on an all-night drinking party in *Who's Afraid of Virginia Woolf?* (Warner Bros., 1966)

wife, while the younger couple who innocently observe their verbal sparring with a mixture of embarrassment and disbelief function as dramatic contrasts to what we witness at center stage throughout the film. The fact that Miss Taylor devotes a great deal of her time to a futile attempt to seduce the young, impressionable Segal underscores not only the significance of her own personal situation but, in a larger sense, the failure of communication, love, and understanding that haunts many contemporary marital relationships as revealed in both serious fiction and dramatic literature. Because of its liberal use of coarse language and sexual innuendo, *Who's Afraid of Virginia Woolf?* is really a landmark of the American movie industry, specifically in its repercussions on the college-life movie tradition. With its release, the movies had taken a considerable leap in their quest for a more expressive and realistic approach to dramatizing human relationships. A masterful stroke on dramatist Albee's part, and one that says more about the modern predicament than anything else in the film, is the ironically negative characterization of one of the most idealistic roles in American professional life—the college teacher. In a larger, more humanistic sense, it is the defeated side of the professor in *Who's Afraid of Virginia Woolf?* which reminds us that there can also be a certain heroism in the passive acceptance of one's fate.

Because of the movies' freer access to dramatizing our mores and social behavior, the college professor as a well-rounded character type was more extensively developed toward the end of the 1960s and on into the 1970s. Major reasons for this new emphasis, of course, were the increased student interest in campus politics (a microcosm, students felt, of politics at large) and the intracampus communication problems that had developed between students and the administration—problems that led to outright confrontation, occasionally culminating in violence and destruction. The generation that came of college age toward the close of the 1960s—the children, in fact, of the G.I. Bill students of the late 1940s—were exposed to a more permissive upbringing and affluent life-style than any generation before it, and came to recognize social reality in an entirely new light. Disenchanted by the many things they saw wrong with society, but particularly irritated by the politics of this country's involvement in the Vietnam war, these students, through their questioning and protesting stance, forced the guardians of academia to look at themselves and their roles from a strikingly different perspective than they ever had before. They also alerted the movie people to the potential dramatic impact of this confrontation. There had been quarrels before, naturally, but never of this order and never on so large a scale. It was most students' contention that this country's involvement in Vietnam was a hopeless cause, since there was no clear-cut justification for our sending troops to this area to begin with. Consequently, anyone or anything related to the support of the war, which of course included the makeup of the American establishment, was subject to attack by militant students who demanded that their concerns be heard.

Traditionally, the college campus has always attracted solitary nonconformists and societal rebels who do not fit into either the academic or social scene, but by the late 1960s, students appeared to be rebelling en masse against the educational establishment. Many of them expressed their criticism and disdain through a variety of ways other than public demonstrations or violence. Shocking personal behavior, reflected primarily through bizarre hair and clothing styles, seemed to be the most popular way in which students rebelled against the middle-class backgrounds and life-styles from which most of them had come. There were other ways, though, some of these even more revolting in their impact on the general public: couples (and groups) cohabitating in open living experimentation; turning on to drugs and narcotics as a communal mode of escapism and fantasizing; a religious devotion to the electronic sounds and enshrined performers of hard-rock music which helped promote their emotional motivation and spiritual solidarity; and a tolerance of and sympathy for anyone or anything that differed from the status quo. Little wonder, then, that the moviemakers recognized in this counterculture movement the dramatic ingredients for visually sensational subject matter. However, as we shall see, not many of their films achieved any level of critical acclaim, even with the supposed advantage of a more liberal approach to interpreting and dramatizing college-life mores.

Most of these films focused on a recurrent campus scene in which frustrated administrators and dismayed, puzzled faculty stood helplessly by while groups of long-haired, pot-smoking, and generally unkempt students turned to overt acts to emphasize their demands. Even F. W. J. "Paco" Perez (Anthony Quinn), the liberal sociology professor of *R.P.M.* (Columbia, 1970), is finally frustrated in his dealings with them. Professor Perez has been something of a culture hero to his students in that he openly vexes the administration of Hudson University through his outspoken liberal views and free-wheeling life-style. It is common knowledge, for example, that Paco makes a practice of selecting one of his students to be his mistress for a quarter, with the intelligent and well-endowed Rhoda Green (Ann-Margret) holding this honor at the time of the story. Because he speaks the students' language and is therefore considered to be in a better position to appease them, the administration accepts one of the student demands that Paco be appointed president of the institution.

In going to such lengths to dramatize the communication gap between the defiant students, who have taken over the administration

By the time of *R.P.M.* (Columbia, 1970), an increasingly liberal attitude toward sexual behavior permitted a scene like this one: a college professor (Anthony Quinn) in bed with one of his students (Ann-Margret).

building, and the self-protective concerns of the faculty and administration, *R.P.M.* implies that the overall institutional problem actually lies beyond the conciliatory powers of Perez. Having gotten the students down from twelve demands to three, Perez discovers that they won't budge from their stand on the last three, among these their threat to smash what they take to be the pervasive symbol of the establishment—the two-million-dollar computer in the administration building. After the police quell the rebellion, Perez realizes for the first time that even he cannot relate to what is happening on the larger scene. His experiences as a radical dissident during the war in Spain and later during the McCarthy era are nothing compared to the issues he now confronts, and Perez admits defeat by walking out, his action symbolizing the communication failure that permeated the collegiate experience during this period. With its delineation of the Perez character, Hollywood had taken the prototype for this kind of role—Professor Turner in *The Male Animal*—to its most extreme portrayal. Turner would have advocated the right of Perez to state his unpopular opinions, but for a professor to openly take a co-ed to his bed would have been an unthinkable social blunder back in the early 1940s.

Another 1970 film, *Getting Straight* (Columbia), focused on the confrontation between the administration and the spokesmen for student grievances through the experience of a graduate student who is studying to become a college teacher. At the age of twenty-eight, Harry Bailey (Elliott Gould) has given up his activist role to join the security of the establishment by becoming a teacher. In his relationship with the faculty and administration, though, Harry discovers that "security" is actually a relative term in its application to the real situation before him. The problem with the faculty and the administration, as Harry sees it, is that they have deceived themselves into thinking that things are better than they are. Even so, Harry acquiesces while his girl friend (Candice Bergen) continues her war with the establishment and looks upon Harry's return to the straight life as a betrayal of principles. Holding down a part-time teaching assignment while working on his degree, Harry tries to warn the faculty of the growing dissent among the students, but to no avail. It is as though his academic associates are in retreat from reality and don't want to hear or believe what he has to say. Finally, after student demonstrations grow into a full-scale riot, Harry rebels against the wavering posture of the faculty and the educational establishment: he

Getting Straight (Columbia, 1970) saw Elliott Gould trying to be a part of the educational establishment but eventually returning to his militant girl friend Candice Bergen when he discovers he cannot be true to himself as a college teacher.

purposely fails his oral exams and returns to the activist pursuits of his girlfriend. The role of Harry Bailey in *Getting Straight*—that of a student-teacher type who is in a position to see both sides of the confrontation—was an excellent choice to dramatize the ambivalence of attitudes toward the American system that existed during this time. The fact that Bailey casts his lot with the dissenters in the end is not so much a turning away from the establishment as it is an acceptance of those who are at least willing to stand up for what they believe in. The college campus has always been a place to test one's ideals, and in the story of Harry Bailey the campus of the late 1960s comes across as a place where the American success ethic was paradoxically reversed, a theme that appears to dominate the college-oriented film of this period.

By 1973 and the release of *The Paper Chase* (20th Century-Fox), things had suddenly settled down on campus and most students appeared to be more concerned with getting good grades than with criticizing their academic leaders. While the development of the story line seems somewhat undecided in *The Paper Chase,* the film achieves its overall dramatic effect through focusing on believable characters. Law student James T. Hart (Timothy Bottoms) is a highly motivated and conscientious scholar from the Midwest who becomes involved in the mad rush for grades at a large eastern law school, ostensibly Harvard. In a classroom relationship that emphasizes the psychological pressures that attend what the students refer to as "the paper chase," Hart is perpetually mystified, repelled, and intrigued by the teaching tactics of his contract law professor, Kingsfield (John Houseman). Apparently to get his points across, Professor Kingsfield engages in an endless series of put-downs and embarrassments of his students. To those of us who have sat under an autocratic teacher it becomes quite clear that Kingsfield as a teacher is strikingly true to the symbolic import of his name: he is an absolute monarch in his classroom kingdom. For the first time in the history of the collegiate film, a serious movie is structured around a professorial character who appears to have the upper hand over his students. Also for the first time, in *The Paper Chase* the movies effectively drew upon the classroom as a compelling dramatic setting in which the natural enmity between student and teacher is played out in an intensely forceful fashion.

There is another side to this clash, too. Kingsfield's daughter, Susan (Lindsay Wagner), to whom Hart is strongly attracted, adds a dimension to the triangular relationship that helps offset the basic conflict between Hart as naïve student and Kingsfield as the symbol of the sophisticated educational system. This conflict may help explain the movie's ambivalent ending: after Hart receives the grades for which he has been working so feverishly, he throws the envelope away unopened. In the long run, the ways of Kingsfield and the system prove unfathomable to Hart, whose attitude toward life demands a natural approach to self-identity. Bottoms performs his role with sensitivity and understanding, and even though *The Paper Chase* might have its dramatic flaws, the acting of the central characters is what holds audience interest. In fact, Houseman's performance came across with sufficient force for him to be nominated for an Academy Award. The road from Fredric March in 1929 as the willy-nilly girl's-school professor in *The Wild Party* had been a long and circuitous one, but movie audiences now recognized that the college professor, when cast in the proper dramatic light, could be a strong presence.[7]

As examples of this conception, other films presented negative portraits of professorial types during this period. Based on the John Barth novel, *The End of the Road* (Allied Artists, 1970), through its focus on a sick and decadent society, apparently tried to dramatize what its title implied about contemporary life. Its antihero (Stacy Keach) has been released from a mental institution to return to teaching at a well-known university, and this film suggests that Keach's societal encounters and relationships are symptomatic of the malaise of modern life. Due to its highly experimental technique (e.g., pe-

Law student Timothy Bottoms and his autocratic professor (John Houseman) wage open warfare in the classroom in *The Paper Chase* (20th Century-Fox, 1973).

riodic montage sequences) and controversial subject matter (e.g., bestiality, frontal nudity, and the social use of drugs), *The End of the Road* was not popularly received, as its mixed reviews indicate. However, *The Hollywood Reporter* thought highly enough of it to categorize it as "art" in that the film "makes a mad merry-go-round of cant, of hypocrisy, or rationalized violence, or glorified stupidity, of sexual hangups, or revolutionary posturing of intellectual know-nothingness."[8] The fact that the contemporary college campus is equated with an insane asylum peopled by inmates who could feel at home in either place stands as the most significant comment in this movie. It is also the first film in the collegiate tradition to be graphic enough to have received an X rating. On a campus where a professor masturbates behind his desk while reading Shakespeare and a co-ed casually rolls a joint during a classroom lecture, the idealized pursuits of the traditional Hollywood collegiate scene appear to be part of another place, another time, making the identification of an institution of higher learning with an insane asylum seem normal enough in *The End of the Road*.

In *The Gambler* (Paramount, 1974), the dark side of contemporary experience is also the inspiration for a film that draws its antihero from academic life. James Caan is college teacher Alex Freed, who, when he is not teaching, busies himself with figuring out ways to satisfy his compulsive gambling habits. Apparently disenchanted with his role as a classroom lecturer—that supposedly rational representative of our social-educational system—Freed searches for the most irrational of experiences and finds it in the psychological intensity of big-time gambling. In fact, his habit becomes intense enough for him to build up a huge gambling debt that forces him to borrow funds from his mother, only to gamble this sum to win and then lose again. Ironically, his indebtedness to the mobsters who are after him for their money brings a reality to his life that Freed has never before experienced, and his existence appears to take on more meaning as a loser or as a prisoner to the gambling system than in any other way, hence the ironic connotation of his name. Even Freed's relationship with a black college basketball player, whom he gets to shave some points in a game, points out his disdain for athletics as a part of the educational system and his romantic outlook on gambling as a way to control the system. In raising a number of important questions about the quality of contemporary society, *The Gambler,* through its dramatic contrast of the reticent role of the academic who abides by the established patterns of the system with the activist role of the gambler who challenges fate to realize individuality, has created a strikingly meaningful metaphor for the modern predicament.

A professorial lead role that had something of a positive definition to it was played by Michael Douglas in the borderline collegiate film

Adam at Six A.M. (National General, 1970). The basic theme of this picture must have been inspired by the rootless and searching mood that characterized the youth of this period. As a newly assigned Ph.D. who is disenchanted with urban life and the abortive demands of the system, Adam Gaines (Douglas) makes up his mind to leave it all behind to search out a more meaningful life-style among the rural people of this country. Although Gaines's story is one of reaction to the contemporary collegiate scene and what it stands for, it also exists as the epitome of the perennial collegiate movie theme that deals with the conflict between an individual's natural outlook and the complex ways of a sophisticated system. *Adam at Six A.M.* can be taken, then, as more than just a marginal film in the collegiate tradition. The seriousness of Gaines's quest is honorable enough (and is what lends this movie something of a sense of purpose on a larger scale), but his efforts are for naught as he eventually discovers that the common moral afflictions of the human condition appear to affect all walks of life. In this modern version of the "American Adam" (the film's title apparently signifies that the hero is at the beginning of his life), Adam Gaines's role is representative of the major contradictions of the 1970s' culture and the pervasive narcissism that seemed to motivate those who were a part of it. The choice of a young, idealistic college professor who rejects his chosen profession to test his own personal code and values is this film's way of telling us where the 1970s might have led us.

Movies that tried to dramatize a positive attitude toward college life from the student's point of view were practically unheard of during this period.[9] In fact, movies that were structured from the special viewpoint of the students during the late 1960s and early 1970s saw something terribly lacking in the efforts of campus administrators to communicate with them, and from the faculty viewpoint these films function as companion pieces to those we looked at earlier. Of these films, the one that most effectively presented the failure and frustrations of the student-establishment conflict was *The Strawberry Statement* (MGM, 1970). Star Bruce Davison, playing the part of a student whose interests reflect those of the average male of the time, at first displays an apathetic attitude toward his fellow students' political demands on the college administration, but through his involvement in a series of demonstrations and sit-ins, he finds himself gradually won over to the student cause. Their posture is most dramatically expressed by the takeover of the dean's office, a symbolic act which, to the students, represents the ultimate coup of the educational establishment. Based on the James Simon Kunen novel about the Columbia University student uprisings of 1969, the movie takes on a visual explicitness that proves to be much more effective than Kunen's fragmented literary method dramatizing his characters' search for self-realization. Through its attempts to put down the authoritarian stance of the administration, combat the thoughtless violence of the police brought in to quell the students' rioting, and indulge in open sex as a form of rebellion (as, for example, a simulated fellatio scene appears to suggest), *The Strawberry Statement*'s overall effect is that of a semi-documentary of the neurotic times that inspired it. Even its musical score, rendered by youth cult figures like Buffy Sainte-Marie, Neil Young, and the musical group Crosby, Stills, Nash, and Young, contributes to both the film's youthful point of view and the disoriented atmosphere of the college campus during this time. The general feeling that movies like *The Strawberry Statement* manage to convey, though, is that of a decided sympathy for the student cause, no matter how radical. The fact that this film was released by Metro-Goldwyn Mayer, that staid old Hollywood studio which had reflected changing public tastes in the movies from its beginnings, reminds us of how far we had come in forty-three years since the comparatively carefree capers of *The Fair Co-ed*.

Another film that drew on the campus unrest of the time to express the theme of alienation not only between students and academia but also as it permeated all walks of contemporary life was Columbia's controversial and puzzling *Drive, He Said* (1971). Directed by the talented but unpredictable Jack Nicholson, this movie depicted the student as drop-out from both school and society in order to get across an obviously embittered assessment of the modern condition.[10] Drawing on the familiar college-life clichés of popular fiction and the movies, particularly those associated with athletics, *Drive, He Said* reverses what one would normally expect of the stock big game situation to express itself instead through shock effect. As a renegade basketball player who continually defies his coach (Bruce Dern), William Tepper has his own ideas about how to play basketball as well as how to relate to society. Thus, in this movie the system of collegiate basketball functions as a comment on society at large, and Tepper's role comes across in a highly paradoxical light when compared to that of Harold Lloyd's eager nonathlete in *The Freshman*. Instead of relishing the popular success that varsity athletics have accorded him, Tepper prefers to buck the demands of the system in order to realize selfhood in a world apparently designed to deny this end. In fact, all of Tepper's social actions, including those of his revolutionary roommate (Michael Margotta), are deliberate taunts in the face of society. For example, Tepper has an affair with a professor's wife (Karen Black) while his roommate affects an insane style of behavior that seems to have no other purpose than to reflect the insanity of the world in which he finds himself. Similar to the enigmatic manner of *The End of the Road* in the previous year, this film's series of chaotic events climaxes with Margotta's final symbolic act before he is

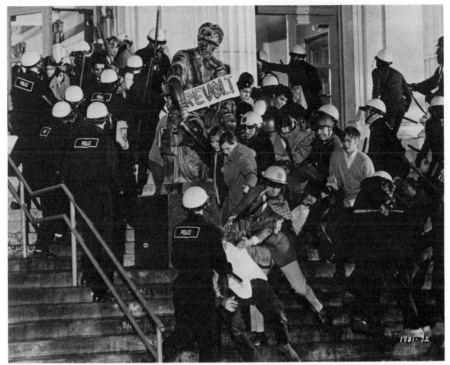

The Strawberry Statement (MGM, 1970), in documenting the Columbia University student riots of 1969, was a vivid contrast to the fantasized social scene depicted in the collegiate films of the 1930s.

hauled away to an asylum: he shows up completely nude at the science building and frees all the experimental insects. In marked contrast to the conventional movie of the collegiate tradition but similar in intent to so many films of this era, *Drive, He Said* leaves the viewer to decide for himself what it may or may not be trying to do or say.

Although the militant movement has since faded, the actions of the students of the 1960s did result in a more democratic representation of students within the administrative structure as well as an accompanying diminishment of administrative autonomy and authority. Even conservative faculty, influenced more than they would care to admit by youthful life-styles, began to think more liberally with respect to the relaxation of academic standards and experimentation with innovative curriculum choices. In spite of these developments, many recent films that have been inspired either partly or entirely by the collegiate experience appear to express a nostalgic feeling for the comparatively serene times before the late 1960s—for example, the 1930s *(The Way We Were)*, the 1940s *(Class of '44)*, the 1950s *(Frater-*

nity Row) and the early 1960s, before the militant movement *(Animal House)*. Apparently, at some point in the 1970s a college-life nostalgia trend set in, portraying the past with its familiar, reassuring images as infinitely more appealing than the present with its unresolved social issues and increasingly confused world outlook.

However, in Paramount's *Fraternity Row* (1977), the past may look interesting enough, but not so much in a nostalgic light, even though the period of the 1950s is authentically visualized. In fact, nostalgia takes a back seat to the satirical intent of this surprisingly mature film, with its bitter attack on the fraternity system of the 1950s —and, by extension, the entire fraternity system as it has always existed. After the militant movement of the 1960s and a concomitant decimation of fraternity membership, the recent revitalization of these social organizations probably played a large part in the decision to make this film about fraternity life as it existed some twenty-five years ago. Bolstered by a strong script and supportive grants, this film is a fine example of the high quality that can be attained on a limited budget with the support of the right movie industry people.[11] With a relatively unknown cast, including Peter Fox, Gregory Harrison, Nancy Morgan, and the late Scott Newman (son of actor Paul Newman), the drama of *Fraternity Row* is expressed through Hollywood's traditional triangular relationship. Newman, a sadistic executor of the hazing rites, is the natural enemy of Harrison, an innocent type who is victimized by the system, while Morgan, Harrison's uncompromising girl friend, tries to warn him of the evils she recognizes in the system before it's too late. All turn in impressively natural performances, but what really makes *Fraternity Row* such an effective movie is its underlying warning to those who would be so narrow-minded as to distort and corrupt the true meaning of brotherhood by giving in to the demands of a system. This message is reinforced by the film's horrifying but compellingly moving ending as we witness what can happen when this message is ignored. Accordingly, *Fraternity Row* implies that the seeds for dissension spread by the elitism and brutal hazing practices of the fraternity system lie dormant and can spring forth at any time with the slightest provocation. Personal ideals as they clash with social reality are significantly presented here in one of Hollywood's most realistic portrayals of the college-life experience.

Because there was such a widespread, almost desperate, search for meaningful involvement and relationships among the college youth of the 1960s and 1970s, romantic love as a serious theme expressed itself in a number of college-oriented films of this era. Some were sincere in dramatizing the motivations for romantic involvement; others merely reiterated the lingering doubts and social confusion that undermined the outlook of youth. *The Young Lovers* (MGM, 1964), for example, deals with the then controversial situation of unmarried college couples making it together, the eventual problem of an unwanted pregnancy, and the question of what to do about it. Due to the moral issue growing out of this predicament, the story intrinsically demands the resolution of its dramatic conflict. Because the key questions are never answered, however, the viewer is left wondering whether the film has any purpose other than to focus on the moral ambivalence of contemporary youth. Peter Fonda is a free-living art student who prefers to keep his life-style unencumbered, even after he impregnates his girl friend (Sharon Hugueny). Since marriage is out of the question for him, he advises an abortion. While the dramatic import of this situation may seem dated by today's standards, the basic moral question of the assumption of responsibility is not. The real significance of *The Young Lovers* is that, along with *Psychomania* of the same year, it is the first collegiate movie to attempt a realistic examination of sexual behavior among college students. What really holds this film back as a mature quality production is its mistaken notion that passion can be comprehended as love, or that sexual promiscuity can develop into the longed-for meaningful relationship. At heart, this same misconception seems to be the inspiration for

Peter Fonda, unwilling to marry, suggests abortion to his co-ed girl friend, Sharon Hugueny, in *The Young Lovers* (MGM, 1964), a film considered bold in its time.

most campus romantic infatuations in the movies at this time.

In support of this assessment, Paramount's *The Sterile Cuckoo* (1969) casts Liza Minnelli as an eccentric, sexually precocious college girl who attracts the affection of a first-year student (Wendell Burton). Her forthright approach to their relationship helps him to overcome his shyness and feelings of inadequacy, with the ironic result that he eventually outgrows her and leaves her behind, both emotionally and literally. Basing its premise on the immature love that can develop between two individuals of college age, this film is both a comment on the failure to communicate and a parable of the eternal but enigmatic relationship between male and female.

The mood was extended satirically to *Carnal Knowledge* (Embassy, 1971), the product of a collaboration between Mike Nichols as director and Jules Feiffer as scriptwriter. They intended to capture on film the chauvinstic methods with which the American male relates to and deals with his women. Beginning in college, where two Amherst roommates (Jack Nicholson and Art Garfunkel) feel compelled to instigate the conquest of a Smith girl (Candice Bergen) in whom they both have a romantic interest, the film follows them on their divergent paths in order to demonstrate how their fouled-up sexual lives actually stem from their expectations for male-female relationships learned in their college days. The film appears to suggest that the superior air cultivated by the college male—symbolized here by the complementary roles of Nicholson and Garfunkel—is, paradoxically, a cover for a basic fear of the female principle and what it stands for: essentially, the social control of the male need for self-expression. The incredibly naïve assumptions about male-female relationships in the college-life movies of the 1930s were now translated in a film like *Carnal Knowledge* as the manifestation of a complex societal attitude controlled by the male, an attitude that dictates the submissive role of women within the system.

On the other hand, *The Harrad Experiment* (Cinema Arts, 1973) attempted to demonstrate what might happen when the standard notions of male-female encounters are challenged by a group of college students engaged in an experimental program. James Whitmore and his wife (Tippi Hedren) are Harrad College professors who are conducting a controlled group project in premarital relations. The students selected for the experiment are to pair off for a month as roommates to see if the possibility of intimate physical relations can result in lasting relationships or just pointless promiscuity. After a series of obviously staged episodes, including a considerable amount of frontal nudity (apparently to suggest current sexual attitudes and hang-ups), the film ultimately makes the point that strong emotional ties between couples are what count, not meaningless affairs. Showing college students in the buff was the most sensational element of this film, and for all its pretense of being a movie that explodes conventional assumptions and attitudes, *The Harrad Experiment* is at heart as old-fashioned as those 1930s romances in which the heroine craftily defends her honor from the advances of the hero to insure the attainment of her ultimate goal—marriage.

Recognizing that young love has always been among the most naturally appealing of dramatic subject matter, the moviemakers have sought to continue the tradition of the collegiate experience as a time-tested and popular backdrop for dramatizing romantic involvement. This situation received its most idealized and polished treatment in Paramount's *Love Story* (1970), which was based on Erich Segal's unabashedly sentimental novel, a runaway best-seller at a time when the general public seemed to be hungering for this particular kind of emotional identification and release. In the manner of the 1930s romantic drama, this film was a box-office hit simply because it turned away from the existing trend toward the sexually explicit and instead concentrated on the humanly emotional, even nostalgic, side of an intense love affair. Actually another variation on the Romeo and Juliet theme, *Love Story* begins with Ryan O'Neal and Ali McGraw meeting in college and discovering that they are from socially differ-

The Harvard-Radcliffe scene provided the backdrop for *Love Story* (Paramount, 1970), which starred Ryan O'Neal and Ali McGraw as author Erich Segal's star-crossed lovers.

ent sides of the tracks: he, of a long-established, prestigious family; she, of a modest, plebeian background. However, this distinction serves mainly to intensify their relationship, and they soon resolve their differences in social status by declaring their love for one another. O'Neal's father (Ray Milland) expects him to finish Harvard Law School and carry on the family firm's name, but he shuns his father's wishes and turns to the girl both his parents feel is beneath his station in life. When O'Neal and Miss McGraw eventually marry, his father disowns him. But the couple go on to their new life together in New York where everything seems to work out fine until O'Neal discovers that his wife is dying, apparently of leukemia. The remainder of the story is built around how the two lovers learn to cope with and accept Miss McGraw's approaching death and O'Neal's beginning a new life with only the memory of her love. Despite a certain contrived manner about Miss McGraw's demise, which leads up to the film's melodramatically sad ending, its depiction of the joys and happiness of young love, however fleeting, comes across as poignantly real. Much of the film's success in conveying this feeling can be attributed to the audience appeal of its college scenes, which obviously are inspired by the college-life movie that dwells on the extracurricular activities of students as opposed to their academic routine. The situation of a rich boy's spoiled outlook tempered and tamed through his association with a basically natural girl's more mature attitudes was also germane to the tradition, but *Love Story* tried to be different by relying on sentiment to complement the social realities of contemporary college life.

By 1977, evolving social attitudes toward questionable language, sexual behavior, and drug use had crystallized in a surprisingly mature movie about a campus romance called *First Love* (Paramount). In fact, what could easily have been turned into an X-rated exploitation film, particularly with respect to its sexual content, was handled tactfully to reveal the deeply human side of two young people discovering the joys and pain of a "first love." William Katt and Susan Dey are the principals, whose quality acting is sufficient to raise the dramatic focus of this film above the level of *Love Story*'s sentimentality, which most audiences of the time were probably conditioned to expect. Meeting first as college students who quickly fall in love, Katt and Dey move through the finer moments of their affair to an eventual breakup caused by Miss Dey's infatuation with an older married man. When she attempts a reunion with Katt, he refuses, recognizing now that their love can never be what it once was and that a first love is usually an emotional experience whose real function is to prepare the participants for what they may romantically encounter in later life. The significance of *First Love* is that it is the first film in the college-life tradition to create both a realistic and meaningful romantic experience out of the more liberal movie code of the 1960s and 1970s.

In the same year, the collegiate movie convention of equating campus romance with athletics was revived in *One on One* (Warner Brothers), a heartwarming but down-to-earth story about a scholarship basketball player's inner conflicts arising out of his love for the game and for his girl. The player is Robby Benson (who, incidentally, collaborated on the script), and the girl is Annette O'Toole, whose effect on Benson's athletic career is to awaken him to the mature outlook that life is more than just a game. Although it depends on the classic clichés of player confronting coach and the last-minute heroic effort, *One on One* ultimately comes across as different from the run-of-the-mill college sports film in that it suggests that the big game is not the end-all but rather a preparation for what is to follow in life. In this movie, viewers discovered that the collegiate sports drama was still very much alive, but dressed up somewhat with a faster-moving sport for a faster moving age.

College-oriented movies like *Love Story, First Love,* and *One on One* reflect the 1970s' infatuation with romantic stories that were sentimental, often realistic, and sometimes even nostalgic. A prime example of the period's growing nostalgia for the way things were— this time, during the war years of the early 1940s—was *Class of '44* (Warner Brothers, 1973), sequel to the box-office hit, *Summer of '42.* A number of reviewers, in fact, charged that the real subject of this picture was not the collegiate experience but nostalgia itself. The lead characters of the earlier success—Hermie, Oscy, and Benjie—are now impelled by the patriotic fervor of their time to enlist in the service, but parental advice dictates draft exemption for Hermie (Gary Grimes) and Oscy (Jerry Houser) through enrollment in college. From this point on, the movie seems obligated to stage a series of period pieces familiar to the collegiate tradition, with the fraternity initiation episode outshining the others in a wonderfully wacky manner that looks ahead to *Animal House* in the late 1970s. Only Hermie's growing emotional involvement with a sorority girl (Deborah Winters) seems to hold the story together, and a serious note is injected with the sudden death of Hermie's father, prompting him to continue his education after he had considered dropping out. In spite of its effective commingling of the comic and the serious, *Class of '44*'s self-conscious focus on period nostalgia turns it into a near parody of the college-life movie of the 1940s.

The year 1973 produced another movie centered around the nostalgic recollection of the collegiate experience, although this film handled the theme in a more realistic fashion. However, the visually fragmented approach to interpreting life in the 1930s and 1940s in *The Way We Were* (Columbia) may make it difficult for viewers to determine just what its theme may be. The dramatic relationship between the lead players (Barbra Streisand and Robert Redford) begins in the 1930s on a college campus where Miss Streisand is active as a political radical and Redford is a big-man-on-campus who obviously enjoys the shallow social life that his popularity has earned him. His talent as a writer assures him of success in later life, but after a promising start as a novelist his career ironically deteriorates into a hack position as a movie scriptwriter. In its portrayal of a type of role peculiar to the 1930s, *The Way We Were* attempts to dramatize what could possibly happen to an individual whose achievements on campus practically guaranteed success in later life. Even after marrying the strong-minded, independent Miss Streisand, who somehow manages to hold on to the political ideals cultivated in her college activist days, Redford continues to be the same self-centered, superficial person he was in college—one who still naturally shrinks from personal problems and complications. When he becomes involved in the political investigations of Hollywood liberals, for example, he gets himself off the hook by cooperating as a friendly witness. Redford's role is a movie variation on the kind of character whom Scott Fitzgerald portrayed so often in his fiction—a personality for whom the only reality, as he grows older, is the nostalgia associated with his past success. Finally realizing that her husband is a weak-willed individual whose way of life is alien to her way of thinking, Miss Streisand walks out on him to pursue her more purposeful goals. The ironic contrast of these two character studies stands as yet another film dramatization of the failure of interpersonal communication in modern life. But through its emphasis on the past as inextricably involved in the process of who and what we become, *The Way We Were* is also a vivid reminder of how influential and affective the college social experience can be in this development. Obviously, the social side of American college life is still looked upon by Hollywood as no less a force in recent years than it was in the 1920s and 1930s, when the movies first began to dramatize their peculiar interpretation of this experience.[12]

While nostalgia has inspired a general aura of sentimental feeling in a number of college-oriented movies of recent years, it has also inspired movies that take an irreverent delight in singling out and deflating those things which have made college life a unique social experience. *Animal House* (Universal City, 1978) returns us to 1962 and the wild goings-on at a Faber College fraternity house during what turns out to be the final semester of its chaotic existence. Espousing a renegade philosophy that not only makes a mockery of the educational establishment but also defies the conventional life-styles and attitudes of the other fraternities on campus, Delta Tau Chi, the "animal house" of the movie's title, practices an anarchistic devotion to revolutionizing the patterns of student behavior through its hedonistic participation in the pleasures of the flesh. In short, the Delts

John Belushi (center) may have stood out among the brothers of *Animal House* (Universal City, 1978), but the real star was the fraternity house itself.

delight in dreaming up ways to make life miserable for the college administration, and for the dean (John Vernon) in particular—the symbol to them of everything the collegiate system stands for. At the same time, Dean Wormer holds no love for the fraternity with the lowest grade-point average on campus and which for years has been the bane of his professional career. As a result, he has sworn to find a way to get the Delts off campus for good. The war between Dean Wormer and the Delts, then, is the basis for the dramatic conflict of *Animal House,* beginning with Rush Week activities in September and ending with the outlawed fraternity's wildly disruptive tactics in the Homecoming parade in November—their last official act as a fraternity but nonetheless a measure of revenge for having been kicked off the campus. The Delts, under the devilishly inspired leadership of members like Bluto (John Belushi), Otter (Tim Matheson), and D-Day (Bruce McGill) prepare for their inevitable demise through a series of events that typically bring no honor to the fraternity but heap much embarrassment on the Faber College administration. Their attitude toward the collegiate system and its leaders peaks in the orgiastic revelry of the toga party where Otter commits the ultimate sacrilege: he takes the dean's drunken wife to bed. In fact, all of the Delts' activities, including the catastrophic grand finale that breaks up the Homecoming parade, appear dedicated to the proposition that nothing really is sacred any more. Like its 1932 forerunner, *Horse Feathers,* this film is in the direct tradition of the college-life movie that finds its source of inspiration in the basically American conflict between authority and self-expression or, as specifically expressed here, through the running feud between the leaders of the educational system and the renegade element of the student body. Even Donald Sutherland's role as a pot-smoking, iconoclastic English professor informs us that the antiestablishment mood is not confined to certain students in this picture, and his character role adds much to the anarchistic aura the film tries to convey. *Animal House* and its outrageous version of disrespect for authority tell us that the socially perceptive tradition of the college-life film is still very much alive.[13]

Reviewing one of the recent films in the collegiate tradition, *Fast Break* (Columbia, 1979), Arthur Knight ironically notes that this movie falls short of "the outrageous kind of college fantasy that Paramount used to produce, with Bing Crosby and Jack Oakie as the perennial undergrads."[14] This observation also falls short because if we look closely for the essential ingredients for this kind of film, we find that they are all intact. *Fast Break* is really Hollywood's collegiate sports movie of the 1930s done all over again for a different age. In fact, the sensational wind-up, in which a castoff bunch of basketball players defeat the best team around, is nothing more than a recreation of the big game focus of the 1930s, and also a pointed reminder that last-minute, heroic efforts have universal, lasting appeal.

The plot of *Fast Break* is basic and simple enough. Gape Kaplan, a familiar comedic image in contemporary television, is cast as a frustrated personality who takes on the basketball coaching job at perennial loser Cadwallader University, where he proceeds to turn a group of New York City street kids into a winning combination. The fact that each team player is a real-life loser unto himself (and herself, since one of the players is a girl who hides her sex from the others) mainly serves to enhance the ultimate significance of the big game when this unlikely combo comes out on top and wins national recognition for the team, the coach, and, of course, the school. Perhaps the *Variety* reviewer of this film is more relevant and perceptive than esteemed critic Knight when he remarks that this movie's "major problem . . . is the absence of that vitality and spark which distinguishes a feature film from its television counterpart. *Fast Break* leaves one waiting for a commercial."[15] Clearly, television has become such a dominant force in current patterns of social behavior

Fast Break (Columbia, 1979), starring TV comedy performer Gabe Kaplan (here, being lifted aloft by his victorious team), demonstrated that the college sports movie of the 1920s and 1930s was still very much alive.

that film viewers are conditioned to expect the characteristic signs of communication that this medium has created.

The college-life movie is still very much the product of conventions as old as the movie industry itself, and like all film traditions that have been created by Hollywood, it is also the composite result of forces greater than the industry itself. As the reviewer of *Fast Break* implied above, television now has a considerable influence on the kind of film that moviemakers think people want and ultimately get. In a day when technological development and expansion can take place almost overnight, and revolutionary social change is very much a fact of life, we have already observed an extensive body of film attesting to Hollywood's interpretation of the impact of technological and social change on contemporary life, including the collegiate experience. Whether they like it or not, our institutions of higher learning have become increasingly involved in the issues and concerns of the complex society they serve; to do so is simply a matter of survival. In recent years, college enrollments among the 18–22-year age group have been dwindling, primarily because the college degree no longer commands the assurance of a promising career that it once did, and also due to the lingering feeling, perhaps more widespread now than ever before, that the halls of academia do little to prepare the individual to confront the complexities of modern life. To combat this attitude, institutions of higher learning have begun to evaluate themselves, their missions, and their roles much more energetically and realistically than they ever have in the past, even going so far as to create a variety of nontraditional missions in their urgent quest to meet the needs of new and different clientele that seem to spring up over night. Their hope is that extended services and the increasing emphasis on the resolution of social problems and special attention to contemporary issues and concerns will help to shatter the public's ivory-tower image of American higher education, and thereby attract nontraditional as well as traditional students. Whatever the outcome, it will be interesting to see how future college-oriented movies react to and interpret this new vision of the American educational mission.

Even so, there is still much that the movies can do with the familiar conventions of the collegiate experience, and a recent film like *Lost and Found* (Columbia, 1979) is exemplary in trying to show what can be done. While it draws on the traditional aspects of the college campus, this film projects them in such a way that they become a microcosm of current psychological uncertainties and economic insecurity. Melvin Frank, the film's producer, director, and coauthor, tried to focus on the trials of the tenure system which most college faculty have had to endure:

> I wanted to say that while most of us think of campuses, the groves of academia, as places of contemplation, of peace and higher thought—the general associations with the collegiate life— nonetheless, there are people basic to that establishment who are suffering terrible economic insecurity. . . . The torture these people go through—the backbiting, the incredible competition and ruthlessness that often exist in what we choose to think of as an atmosphere of contemplation and peace—is subject matter that I don't believe has ever been used properly, if at all, on the screen.[16]

George Segal is a college professor at a small New England school who is under pressure to finish his doctoral dissertation in order to obtain tenure. A variety of problems keep him from achieving his goal: a domineering mother (Maureen Stapleton) who believes her son is too good for the position he holds, an attractive co-ed (Hollis McLaren) obviously on the make, and competition from a rival instructor (John Cunningham). But Segal's major roadblock materializes in the person of his newly acquired bride (Glenda Jackson). Playing the role of an Italian film producer's ex-wife, Miss Jackson brings an air of sophistication to the campus which doesn't fit into the established scheme of things. In fact, she comes across as the natural enemy of the status quo, rubbing Segal's faculty peers the wrong way and putting down a film critic who has been invited to campus as a guest lecturer. In a paradoxical sense, Miss Jackson's role is a reversal of the collegiate film's favorite plot situation of the naïve newcomer confronting the system, for her worldly-wise ways serve to offset the retreat from the real world that has always been a distinctive feature of the traditional collegiate experience. The contrast between Miss Jackson's critical, forthright outlook and the passive, cloistered posture of Segal accounts for both the film's comic perspective and its serious side. Ultimately, *Lost and Found* comes across as the story of two individuals learning how to communicate within the rigid expectations of an unfathomable social system.

In spite of the state of flux in which the institution of higher learning finds itself today, it would appear that the primary role and scope of American education will continue to be tempered by the cultural ideals and social goals of the individual. The democratization of the educational process has reached the point today where higher education has begun to address the unique needs of specially defined groups more intensely than it ever has before. This situation in itself is prime enough to invite the attention of the movie people. It remains to be seen, however, to what extent the future student's sensitivity to social reaction and rebellion will be tested in the environs of the traditionally conservative, yet increasingly liberal and condescending, American college or university. Whatever happens, we can rest assured that the movies will dramatize their peculiar version of it. Melvin Frank's perceptive remarks on the thorns in the "groves of academia" remind us that the tradition of the college-life movie, like that of any popular film genre, will continue as long as the creative eye can determine what is significant and meaningful within the ongoing drama of human relationships.

Notes

1 Origins: The Collegiate Experience and the World of the College-Life Movie

1. Ethel Clayton performed the first college-widow movie role in 1915. Basically, the "college widow" theme was a variation of the triangular plot that so many college-life film plays were dependent upon. In this particular case, the heroine divides her attentions between the college, which is her real love, and the team players instead of between two competing beaus. For further discussion of the triangular plot, see pp. 17–18.

2. In this film, the comic emphasis on misdirected social behavior as well as surprising turns of plot affords us a preview of the popular screwball comedy genre of the 1930s. Incidentally, a future star of this kind of movie, Loretta Young, made her screen debut in *Naughty but Nice* in 1927. That year saw several other future stars appearing in college-life movies: Jean Arthur in *The Poor Nut* (First National), Claudette Colbert in *For Love of Mike* (First National), and Jason Robards in *White Flannels* (Warner Bros.).

3. Most often, though, it is the student who lacks financial support and social standing that commands our empathy—someone like football star Richard Dix in *The Quarterback* (1926), for example, who works his way through the conventional four years of college by delivering milk in the early morning hours.

4. The athlete as a symbol of individualized expression within the system was also romanticized by both Fitzgerald and Marks. But as fictional and movie roles have reflected changing values over the years, the athlete came to be frequently depicted as selling out to the system while the college professor eventually came across as a symbol of individual integrity in the face of hypocrisy and conformity. Undoubtedly, the increasing professionalism of the college athlete has undermined his fictional and film image since the 1920s.

5. The movies' portrayal of the College Man type, in ranging from worldly-wise sophisticate to antiestablishment radical or carefree party boy, reveals how students' codes of dress have reflected the changing tastes and values that would ultimately evolve into the iconoclastic behavior of the 1960s. During this time undergraduates, in their complete disregard for traditional styles of dress and appearance, actually started the fashion of *no* fashion, a mode still very much with us but which has become in its way just as affected as any previous style of collegiate dress.

6. This traditional weekend celebration is climaxed, of course, by a football game in which the home team takes on a rival whose defeat is imperative. Past records, national recognition, or

a bowl bid do not matter so much as does victory in this one game. Even though the honor of the school may be at stake, the movies' focus on the big game makes it quite clear that the real honor in question is that of a film's central figure. For example, in *College Days* (Tiffany, 1926), hero Charles Delaney is called into the big game at the last minute to help his team win—an accomplishment that improves his shaky relationship with both the school officials and his girl friend. Undoubtedly, the most sensational appearance at a big game finale was pulled off by Johnnie Walker in *Live Wires* (Fox, 1921). Upon his release from jail, Walker boards a train that proves to be too slow to get him to the game on time, so he climbs up on the roof of the speeding train where a plane whisks him away to the stadium!

7. Over the years, the University of Notre Dame has persisted as the real-life embodiment of the spirit of the big game and as such has established the dramatic model for the movies to draw upon, which indeed they have done, producing pictures as disparate in intent as the controversial *John Goldfarb, Please Come Home* (20th Century-Fox, 1965) and the outstanding bio-pic, *Knute Rockne, All-American* (1940). Despite the cross-purposes of these two films, one seemingly denigrating and the other obviously elevating the Notre Dame mystique, both are equally dependent on its basic significance to get their points across.

8. Paddock, who appeared in a number of collegiate films, played himself in *The Olympic Hero* (Supreme, 1928), which contained footage of the 1924 Olympics. In *Swim, Girl, Swim* (Paramount, 1927), swimmer Gertrude Ederle helps co-ed Bebe Daniels become a champion swimmer in order to impress her boy friend. Numerous other popular films, unrelated to the college-life tradition, featured super athletes of the era like Jack Dempsey and Babe Ruth.

9. Considered to be one of the greatest collegiate football players of all time, Harold (Red) Grange played for Illinois during 1923–25. He had his greatest day on October 18, 1924, against Michigan, when in the space of twelve minutes he ran for four touchdowns in the opening quarter. Grange had handled the ball only four times on long scoring runs. He was taken out of the game but returned in the second half to score a touchdown and pass for another.

10. From the *Variety* review of *The Quarterback* (13 October 1926).

11. A little known point of information about this film is that John Wayne (Marion Morrison), fresh off the Southern California campus, is supposed to have made his first movie appearance by doubling for Bushman in some football action scenes.

12. Even though Joan Crawford had just established herself as a promising newcomer in *Our Dancing Daughters* (MGM, 1928), *The Duke Steps Out* was considered a reversal of form for her. In fact, one reviewer went so far as to assert that she would have to make up a lot of lost ground in her next film if she was to go "anywhere in a fast moving field that's now moving faster." (*Variety*, 17 April 1929) Miss Crawford obviously got the message, as she was soon recognized as one of Hollywood's biggest stars.

13. Evidently this film was popular enough to demand a remake in 1928 as *Red Lips* (Universal), starring Marion Nixon, Buddy Rogers, and Andy Devine.

14. The expression "long line" prompts the gossip that Miss Bow was rumored to have had a special fondness for University of Southern California football players with whom, it was said, she extended her collegiate allegiance beyond that of just her filmmaking.

15. As if in reaction to the posture of *The Wild Party*, First National came out with *Hot Stuff* in the same year. Alice White is a college girl who tries her hand at a swinging life-style only to discover in the end that it is the virtuous girl whom the guys really want.

16. From the *Variety* review of *The College Hero* (23 November 1927).

17. Ironically, this film was remade and released under the identical title in the same year as *The Freshman* (1925).

18. One of the more interesting variations was *The College Boob* (Film Booking Office, 1926), whose reluctant hero has promised his folks that he will not participate in sports, even though he does have athletic ability. Ridiculed as the "college boob," he ultimately wins his classmates' respect when he becomes the hero of the big football game.

19. Ironically, Keaton, who usually insisted on performing his own stunt work, hired an athlete to double for him on this feat.

20. This film was remade in 1925 and retitled *Braveheart*.

21. Another college-oriented racial theme was expanded upon in an early sound film, *Redskin* (Paramount, 1929), which had Richard Dix playing an Indian athlete whose collegiate career informs him that it's apparently a white man's world. He returns to his tribe to win over his childhood sweetheart, who had been promised in marriage to the heavy of this triangular plot. However, it is Dix's background in the white man's world that urges him and his new wife to set out on their own toward a new life. That black-white relationships were not unknown to Hollywood at this time was attested by the appearance in 1921 of *The Burden of Race* (Reol), which tells the story of a black student falling in love with a white girl.

22. This conflict had been intimated in a film like *Readin', 'Ritin', 'Rithmetic* (Artlee, 1926) in which a professor frowns upon his daughter dating the college athletic hero, whose scholarly interests fall considerably below the professor's standards.

23. The ending of *College* is comprised of an abrupt series of dissolves which show Ronald and Mary happily married with their children, next as an old couple, and then two tombstones, as if to question the meaning and purpose of life's way of involving us with our destinies.

2 Variations: The 1930s

1. *The Forward Pass,* naturally, was a football story in which Douglas Fairbanks, Jr. is a pass-happy star player who brings his team back in the final quarter of the big game, but only after straightening out his favorite pass receiver and discovering that contentious co-ed Loretta Young is really very much on his side. As a teenager near the start of her long career, Miss Young even manages to sing a song in this feature.

The triangular plot of *So This Is College* has Robert Montgomery and Elliott Nugent as two football players who finally come to the realization that the girl of their dreams has been deceiving both of them. Luckily, the boys get their act together just in time to win the big game in the second half.

Words and Music, which featured John Wayne (listed in the credits as Duke Morrison) in one of his earliest roles, was a twist on the "let's-put-on-a-show" situation, with collegians competing for a money prize for producing the best musical.

In *Sweetie,* Nancy Carroll, Stu Erwin, and Jack Oakie find their lives becoming more complicated when Miss Carroll inherits a college campus.

2. From the *Variety* review of *Varsity* (31 October 1928).

3. From the *Variety* review of *So This Is College* (13 November 1929).

4. Other Hollywood musicals with a collegiate theme during this period were *Howdy Broadway* (Rayart, 1929), a curious blend of college life and the bright lights of New York; *The Time, the Place, the Girl* (Warner Brothers), which featured the popular song, "Collegiate"; *Cheer Up and Smile* (Fox), starring Bing Crosby's first wife Dixie Lee; and *Sunny Skies* (Tiffany), which involved Rex Lease in another triangular predicament.

5. From the *Variety* review of *College Humor* (27 June 1933).

6. In *The Sweetheart of Sigma Chi,* Betty is featured with Ted Fio Rito's orchestra in a song-and-dance routine. With a plot that lacked any dramatic conflict whatsoever, this film's only noteworthy features were its male lead—former Olympic swimmer Larry "Buster" Crabbe—a lilting, catchy title tune, and the fact that it devotes one of its sequences to the classroom, a rare occurrence in the college-life film of this era.

In *Student Tour,* Betty is among a group of students on a round-the-world cruise directed by a couple of madcap tour leaders: crew coach Jimmy Durante and crackpot philosophy prof Charles Butterworth, whose role helped reaffirm the public's innate suspicion of the academic type. After a number of tour stops, which actually function as weak excuses for musical productions, the cruise ends in typical big game fashion with a crew race against England on the Thames River, but for most audiences the picture had ended much earlier. Although the talented team of Nacio Herb Brown and Arthur Freed composed the film's tunes (which, incidentally, spotlight an early screen appearance of singer Nelson Eddy), the appealing music unfortunately isn't enough to rescue this film from oblivion.

Old Man Rhythm wasn't much better fare, but the casting found Miss Grable moving up a notch or two closer to the male lead—this time Charles "Buddy" Rogers, another of the day's popular romantic crooners. As a variation of the rich-boy theme, the story has Buddy as a campus playboy whose roving disposition has played havoc with his grades. To get the delinquent student back on the right track, his father decides to enroll as a freshman. This situation helped vary the social side of this kind of movie and made for a few laughs, but the picture turned out to be one of the weaker college-life vehicles of the day.

7. From the *Variety* review of *College Rhythm* (27 November 1934).

8. The problems encountered by a star player and the doubt as to whether or not he would be able to perform in the big game were so obligatory to collegiate films of the 1930s that critics, in their eagerness to find something original about them, would praise films like MGM's *Spring Madness* (1938) for completely ignoring the cliché ending through simply concentrating on romantic comedy capers without making any reference to sports whatsoever.

9. On the credit side, these three films did strive for original story lines but ultimately failed in arousing sufficient audience interest. In *Bachelor of Arts,* Tom Brown is a rich-boy collegian who is continually in trouble, but his concerned girl friend (Anita Louise) puts him to the test when she gets his dad to fake the loss of his millions.

Instead of football, the sport in *Freshman Love* is rowing, and the coach of Billings College, played by Frank McHugh, won't keep his job unless he can turn out a winning crew. Naturally, the president's daughter (Patricia Ellis) uses her charms to recruit talented material, but Coach McHugh complicates the plot by sending out letters that include her picture to potential crewmen.

In *Over the Goal,* the football hero (William Hopper) has promised his girl (June Travis) that he won't play any more football lest he wind up with a disabling injury. Hopper is faced with a dilemma, though, when he discovers that his college stands to inherit a large sum of money if the team can defeat its big rival, but his own family stands to win if his team loses. Needless to say, Hopper casts his lot with his school and arrives at the game in time to win the legacy for his alma mater. Apparently, to vary the big-game formula, scriptwriters of the 1930's were inspired to characterize athletes as occasionally motivated by higher values than just playing for self.

10. An interesting aside concerning *Start Cheering* is its ambivalent attitude toward the relationship of education and athletics. The situation of Charles Starrett forsaking a well-paying career for a college education, yet recognizing the social importance of participating in athletics, reflected the Hollywood understanding that it could debunk the clichés surrounding athletic activity but not athletics itself. The educational system, however, was still fair game, and the appearance of the Three Stooges in several slapstick routines in this film undoubtedly had an effect on the public's opinion about the caliber of people one meets at college in much the same way that the Marx Brothers had conditioned earlier audiences.

11. Incidentally, Marshall Neilan, the director of *Swing It, Professor,* had appeared in a principal role in one of the earliest collegiate films, *Classmates* (Biograph, 1914).

12. Yankee Stade, "Football—A $50,000,000 Business," *Liberty* 15, no. 40 (1 October 1938), pp. 11–12.

13. Once again, the team of Mack Gordon and Harry Revel contributed to the musical side of a college-life film, and Marjorie Weaver and Jack Haley (on his way to being immortalized in *The Wizard of Oz*) turned in attractive supporting performances. An interesting sidelight, attesting to Hollywood's stereotyping of educators as reticent, passive personalities, was the casting of the mousy Donald Meek as an obsequious college president who is influenced in his decisions by his political connections.

14. The practice of signing real-life sports people to the movies hit a high in the 1930s with the frequent contracting of entire teams as, for example, several squads from the University of Southern California during the decade.

15. In a humorous vein, the sexual connotation of this film's title might have been somewhat misleading to some moviegoers, as this movie, like most football dramas, was low in suggestive content. Also noteworthy is the fact that both John Wayne and Ward Bond had minor roles as players on the same team.

16. Another Wallace story, *That's My Boy,* was produced by Columbia in the same year as *Huddle.* Not to be confused with the Martin and Lewis vehicle of the 1950s, this movie starred Richard Cromwell as a football star who finds his athletic career in jeopardy as the result of his involvement in a phony stock-selling scheme.

17. Because of the popular practice of signing well-known football stars to the movies, many youths of the 1930s must have concluded that one sure way to get to Hollywood and the movies was to become a football star.

18. From the *Variety* review of *The All-American* (4 October 1932).

19. The popular image of the coach was reinforced in this movie as five well-known mentors of the day put in an appearance along with the usual lineup of all-American players like Biggie Munn, Chris Cagle, Ernie Nevers, Frank Carideo, and Albie Booth. The coaches—among them, W. A. Alexander of Georgia Tech, Jesse Harper of Notre Dame, and Pop Warner of Stanford—were members of what was referred to then as the "All-American Board of Football." Their primary mission was to pick an all-star team every year for a newspaper syndicate, and one of this film's sequences shows them in the act of making their choices. An effective gimmick at this time, it must have inspired a multitude of young boys who saw this scene to feel that they could someday be named to this dream team themselves.

20. From the *Variety* review of *Saturday's Millions* (17 October 1933).

21. From the *Variety* review of *The Big Game* (28 October 1936).

22. The threadbare plot of *Rose Bowl* has grid stars Brown and Benny Baker enduring a pitifully anemic social life due to big-man-on-campus Buster Crabbe's cornering the co-ed market. When Crabbe eventually gets his comeuppance, Brown and Baker improve their social standing with the girls. Buster Crabbe had better things awaiting him just around the corner in the role of comic-strip hero Flash Gordon in the Universal serials with which he would be henceforth associated. Coincidentally, Priscilla Lawson, who would win the part of the Emperor Ming's daughter, made one of her first movie appearances in *Rose Bowl.*

23. From the *Variety* review of *Swing That Cheer* (10 November 1938).

24. From the *Variety* review of *The Band Plays On* (25 December 1934).

25. From the *Variety* review of *So This Is College* (13 November 1929).

26. From the *Variety* review of *Over the Goal* (6 October 1937).

27. The fact that college-life movies of the 1930s, like *$1,000 a Touchdown,* interpreted athletics as highly essential to the educational process is really not so farfetched, even in our own day. In a 1980 news release, Florida State University attributed a significant increase in their freshman class enrollment during a time of nationally declining enrollment to the overall success of their 1979–80 athletic programs, which were among the nation's best.

28. In *Local Boy Makes Good,* Brown inadvertently qualifies as a dash man on the college track team when he has to run for his life after nearly killing the team captain with a javelin. Like Keaton, Brown was at his athletic best during moments of dire emergency.

29. This observation is further substantiated by *Girls Demand Excitement* (Fox, 1931), an inane comedy that would have come off much better as a musical. Here the old battle-of-the-sexes theme is extended to the basketball court, where the girls take on the boys to decide a campus issue. Of interest to film buffs is the fact that this movie was an early vehicle for John Wayne, who took second billing to a now forgotten actress named Virginia Cherill. Wayne later identified this movie as his worst, including all those B Westerns he made during the 1930s.

A Damon Runyan story contained yet another version of the influence of women on college athletics in the film adaptation of *Hold 'em Yale* (Paramount, 1935), not to be confused with the same title produced by Pathé in 1928, starring Rod La Roque. In the Runyan story, two of his shady but likable street characters, played by Andy Devine and William Frawley, attempt to pair off their boss's delinquent daughter with a Yale football player (Buster Crabbe), with some mildly amusing results.

30. Another variation on the theme was the Cinderella situation of a girl courted by a professor in United Artists' 1939 entry in the college-life derby, *Winter Carnival.* In this romantic comedy, Ann Sheridan is the girl and Richard Carlson the professor who come to know each other more intimately as a result of their meeting during a weekend modeled after the Dart-

mouth College festivities of the film's title. Incidentally, this is the film on whose script F. Scott Fitzgerald collaborated with Budd Schulberg, inspiring Schulberg's portrait of an alcoholic writer in his novel, *The Disenchanted*.

Another film based on the student-professor romance was *Girls' Dormitory* (20th Century-Fox, 1936), a melodrama with a European setting. Here student Simone Simon supposedly falls for headmaster Herbert Marshall, whom she deceives in the end for a youthful Tyrone Power. Most movies in which co-eds carry on affairs with their professors, like *Girls' Dormitory*, come across as soap-opera vehicles in which conventional campus behavior is self-consciously defied.

31. Paramount had already made a film in 1932 with the title *Million Dollar Legs*, which featured W. C. Fields as the president of a mythical country with Olympic aspirations.

32. Columbia contributed its version of this kind of film with *Campus Mystery* (1938), but it was noticeably lacking in the qualities of the two films cited here.

33. From *The New York Times* review of *Confessions of a Co-ed* (20 June 1931).

34. From the *Variety* review of *Age of Consent* (6 September 1932).

35. In 1921, Warner Brothers had made a film with a plot similar to that of *Sorority House*. Titled simply *Ashamed of Parents*, the Warner story told of a football hero who rejects his poor father who has spent his life's savings to send his son to college.

36. Anne Shirley, the lead in *Sorority House*, had also starred in a school-oriented picture in 1938 called *Girls' School* (Columbia), a surprisingly entertaining B film in which Miss Shirley and one of her teachers conspire against their school's regulations to elope with their boyfriends.

37. Incidentally, one of the more familiar faces of the 1940s—Veronica Lake—first made her screen appearance as one of the co-eds in *Sorority House*.

38. From the *Variety* review of *Classmates* (31 December 1924).

39. From the *Variety* review of *The Midshipman* (14 October 1925).

40. In actuality, the period 1925–30 reflects a fairly even spread in movies inspired by either a West Point or an Annapolis background. In contrast to those films which opted for this kind of setting, like *Annapolis* (Pathé, 1928) starring Johnny Mack Brown, one movie created its own military setting: *Eyes Right!* (Goodwill, 1926), a Francis X. Bushman vehicle in which he attends the "San Diego Army and Navy Academy," a name which obviously addressed the interests of each side.

41. Speaking of originality, Universal's *The Flaming Frontier* (1926) would undoubtedly take the prize among military school offerings. In 1921, there was *False Women* (Aycie) which tells of a priest going to college, and in 1922, *The Freshie* was built around a cowboy's experiences at college, but *The Flaming Frontier* had cowboy Hoot Gibson attending West Point. After being kicked out when he takes the blame for a scandal of which he is innocent, he serves under General Custer, is cleared of all charges, and returns to West Point as a hero.

42. From the *Variety* review of *Salute* (21 August 1929). But by the 1930s the clichés of the military school drama were beginning to wear thin as evidenced by a *Variety* review of *Midshipman Jack* (RKO, 1933). Starring Bruce Cabot, this film depicts him as the familiar character who "gets in dutch with the regulations and almost loses his chance at a commission, only to become heir to a halo and marry the commandant's daughter." Increased critical demands are reflected in the reviewer's observation that the movie is "splendidly photographed, but it takes more than photography these days." (21 November 1933)

43. Paramount extended its peculiar feel for the genre with *Annapolis Farewell* (1935), *Hold 'em Navy* (1937), and *Touchdown Army* (1938) while Universal turned out *Naval Academy* (1941).

44. *A Yank at Oxford* inspired two other spinoffs—*A Chump at Oxford* (United Artists), a 1940 vehicle for comics Stan Laurel and Oliver Hardy, and *A Yank at Eton* (MGM), in which Mickey Rooney plays a junior version of Robert Taylor's earlier role.

3 Extensions: The 1940s–1950s

1. From the *Variety* review of *Knute Rockne—All-American* (9 October 1940).

2. In 1943, during the peak of the war years, O'Brien would play another dynamic coaching personality in *The Iron Major* (RKO), the story of Frank Cavanaugh, a World War I hero whose screen biography brought inspirational comfort to many audiences during the dark days of WW II.

3. In 1941 there was *Harmon of Michigan* (Columbia), which concentrated on all-American Tom Harmon's experiences after college graduation. The following year, Columbia produced two more of the same type of film: *The Spirit of Stanford* with real-life quarterback Frankie Albert performing in a role right out of the 1930s (he overcomes his cocksure manner to win the big game), and *Smith of Minnesota,* which introduced a unique approach to the genre by having an investigative reporter visit all-American Bruce Smith's home town to uncover the events that led to his football fame.

4. Much of the emphasis on the spirit theme in literature and related subject matter in the early part of this century is attributable to Teddy Roosevelt's manly code of behavior, which preached a patriotic devotion to what this country was supposed to stand for. It was a feeling especially common around the time of World War I when author F. Scott Fitzgerald—in all seriousness, but apparently under the spell of the juvenile fiction he had read in his youth—could emote that heroic deeds on the football field and the battlefield complemented each other. Thus it was naïvely assumed that one's allegiance to his alma mater should inspire dedication to country, a type of spiritual enthusiasm symbolized by a motto like that of Yale University: "For God, for country, and for Yale." As we have seen, this religious attitude or spirit pervaded and colored the atmosphere of a plethora of movies like *Brown of Harvard* (1926), *Maker of Men* (1931), *The Spirit of Notre Dame* (1931), and, of course, the best example, *Knute Rockne—All-American* (1940).

5. Marty Maher's civilian counterpart in the movies was captured most appealingly in the British role of Mr. Chips from James Hilton's novel, *Goodbye, Mr. Chips.* Thirty years after Robert Donat's performance in 1939, Peter O'Toole would portray the beloved schoolmaster who became a legend to several generations of boys at a British prep school.

6. *The Jackie Robinson Story* (Eagle-Lion, 1950) dramatized the life of the all-round UCLA athlete who became the first black player in major-league baseball, while *Jim Thorpe, All-American* (Warner Brothers, 1951) told the story of the Carlisle College American Indian (Burt Lancaster) who was charged with professionalism and stripped of his Olympic medals. A comparatively straightforward presentation of a real-life personality was Republic's *Crazylegs* (1953), which concentrated on the professional football career of Wisconsin all-American, Elroy "Crazylegs" Hirsch.

7. See "University Days" from Thurber's *My Life and Hard Times* (New York: Harper & Bros., 1933).

8. Alexander Knox plays the role of the English instructor in a curiously ambivalent manner, openly displaying his distaste for the athletic type while singling out Steve Novak in class for his superior academic ability.

9. Another attempt to humanize the life of a college football player was Monogram's *The Rose Bowl Story* (1952), but Marshall Thompson comes across as just another jock in a long line of such characters. This film also continued the notion that football is more a form of entertainment than it is an athletic event. Vera Miles, Natalie Wood, and Jim Backus played supporting roles in this film that relied on its title more than anything else to promote it.

10. From *The Hollywood Reporter* review of *Bathing Beauty* (26 May 1944).

11. In her rush toward popular acclaim, Lucille Ball would go on to MGM, where she would make an appealing musical with a military prep-school background—*Best Foot Forward* (1943), which was highlighted by the definitive spirit song, "Buckle Down Winsocki."

12. In one of the more successful Hollywood marital matches, Harriet Hilliard married Ozzie

Nelson, and they went on to become the stars of the most popular family television series of the 1950s—*Ozzie and Harriet.*

13. Also deserving mention as lending to the overall quality of *Sis Hopkins* is the casting of young Susan Hayward and Bing Crosby's brother Bob, whose orchestra, the Bob Cats, performed a score turned out by the talented team of Jule Styne and Frank Loesser.

14. Two other outstanding B musicals of the 1940s were *Zis Boom Bah* (Monogram, 1941) and *Campus Rhythm* (Monogram, 1943). In the earlier film, education and entertainment come together again when the talented family team of Grace Hayes, Peter Lind Hayes (Grace's son), and Mary Healy (Peter's wife) find themselves resolving family problems within a collegiate background. *Campus Rhythm* structured its musical productions around the singing-dancing abilities of Gale Storm, another popular B movie performer who would go on to make a name for herself in television situation comedies of the 1950s. In this movie, Gale forsakes a radio career to enroll as an unknown in a small college. After a series of complications generated by Robert Lowery and Johnny Downs, she gives in to the old college spirit, reveals her true identity, and helps put her school on the map.

15. From *The Hollywood Reporter* review of *Sweater Girl* (5 May 1942).

16. The influence of *Brother Rat* cropped up again in 1958 in the popularly received *Mardi Gras* (20th Century-Fox). In this picture Pat Boone, Tommy Sands, and Gary Crosby are cadets at Virginia Military Institute where they come up with the idea of conducting a raffle, the winner to receive a date with a beautiful French movie star (Christine Carere) who is to be queen of the Mardi Gras celebration in New Orleans. As members of VMI's band and color guard, all the principals show up in New Orleans, where a torrid romance develops between raffle winner Boone and Miss Carere. Two members of her entourage, Sheree North and Fred Clark, complicate matters by attempting to break up the affair. But it is Bing's son Gary who steals the show with his version of the affable Crosby manner. As one of the last innocent romps before students' questioning and protesting attitudes of the 1960s, *Mardi Gras* commands a great deal of audience appeal, mainly because of its excellent on-site photography at both VMI and in New Orleans, proving what the movies can do best—mix reality with fantasy.

17. Two 1941 B movies worthy of mention—*All-American Co-ed* (United Artists) and *Let's Go Collegiate* (Monogram)—put the dual or mistaken-identity convention to entertaining use. The former film had Johnny Downs as a "Quinceton" man in drag, entered by his fraternity brothers in a rival girls' school beauty contest in order to gain revenge for an affront to Quinceton. This was another of Hal Roach's many shorter length films designed for double-bill presentation.

Let's Go Collegiate saw Frankie Darro, Jackie Moran, and Keye Luke recruiting a bank robber as the replacement for a member of the crew team who's been drafted. There are some anxious as well as naturally comic moments as the fugitive from justice performs admirably for the boys' school, even helping to win the big race. But when the old grads find him out, he winds up being carted off to jail according to the dramatic code of the time. Supported by the singing talent of Gale Storm and the comedy antics of Mantan Moreland, a black actor who never appeared to be bothered by racial concerns, *Let's Go Collegiate* was a pleasant surprise for moviegoers. In time, the medium of television would begin identifying these short features as "situation" comedies.

18. The professorial type and his relationship with women have provided the source of inspiration for a number of noncollegiate films including *I'll Show You the Town* (Universal, 1925), in which the social instincts of a college instructor are put to the test when he entertains three different female personalities at the same time; and *Ball of Fire* (RKO, 1941), in which Gary Cooper is a bumbling linguist who gets mixed up with the gangland connections of Barbara Stanwyck—another twist on *The Blue Angel* theme.

19. In *It Happens Every Spring,* Ray Milland is cast as a mild-mannered college professor who comes up with a formula that makes baseballs "allergic" to wood. Because he is financially unable to marry his girl friend (Susan Peters), Milland leaves his research position to become a pitcher for the St. Louis baseball team. In this capacity, his invention allows Milland to win some of the most sensational and wackiest games ever played—thanks to the highly entertaining

special effects of this film. After losing his formula, Professor Milland is allowed to return to his college position, now wealthy enough to marry his girl.

20. An earlier, more serious variation on the failure of relationships in a college-oriented family was *Young Ideas* (MGM, 1943), whose script, incidentally, had been written by an undergraduate. The story, which has soap-opera overtones, concerns itself with a novelist (Mary Astor) and her affair with a college professor (Herbert Marshall) whom she eventually marries, much to the disapproval of her children (Susan Peters and Elliott Reid), who are students of the professor's.

21. Another film that treated a woman academic type in a sympathetic light was *Do You Love Me* (20th Century-Fox, 1946), a musical which cast beautiful Maureen O'Hara as the strait-laced dean of a music college. On a trip to New York to recruit a conductor for her school's music festival, Miss O'Hara is confronted by the popular singing style of Dick Haymes and the big-band sound of Harry James and his Music Makers. Initially turned off, Dean O'Hara inevitably undergoes a Cinderella transformation that endears her to both her associates in the film and to audiences.

22. The precedent for an older woman returning to school was set in *Only 38* (Famous Players, 1923) when Lois Wilson, the mother of college boys, starts to work as a college librarian and is inspired to change her life-style to keep pace with her collegiate environment.

23. Originally titled *At Good Old Siwash, Those Were the Days* was based on the college-life stories of George Fitch, who is credited with creating that paragon of fictional collegiate institutions—Siwash College.

24. Cornelia Otis Skinner, actress, and Emily Kimbrough, writer, were classmates at Bryn Mawr College in the early 1920s, an experience that provided much of the autobiographical background for their books.

25. *The Collegians* proved to be popular enough as a series that Universal pieced a number of these shorts together in a feature-length movie that appeared in 1929 as *College Love*. Because this series spanned the era of the silents and the beginning of sound, *College Love,* interestingly enough, was only 50 percent talking.

26. After a real-life hitch in the Army, Mickey Rooney returned in 1946 to appear in *Love Laughs at Andy Hardy,* the third college-oriented movie in this series. In this one, though, college is just a backdrop for Andy's immediate problem—a breakup with his love interest of the previous film, Bonita Granville. Actually, Rooney was getting too old for the Andy Hardy role by this time in his career, and this movie began to show the frayed edges of an overworked formula. Due to their popularity, though, the Andy Hardy series went a long way in perpetuating the notion that the collegiate experience is nothing more than learning how to get along socially.

27. Even comic-strip characters that the movies had parlayed into series feature films got into the collegiate act when, in 1942, Chic Young's widely syndicated newspaper comics creation, "Blondie," was allowed to experience the joys of higher education in *Blondie Goes to College* (Columbia). As the family orientation of this series permitted the whole Bumstead clan to participate in any action that Blondie got involved with, her husband Dagwood enrolls in school too, and, true to formula, winds up as a bumbling football player. Penny Singleton always turned in a creditable performance in the lead role of this series, and Arthur Lake as Dagwood even managed to resemble his comic-strip counterpart.

From popular fiction came Michael Arlen's super sleuth, the Falcon, played by suave Tom Conway, in an entertaining murder mystery called *The Falcon and the Co-eds* (RKO, 1943). There are the usual stock portrayals of the students and academicians, but the plot is suspenseful enough to hold interest until the very last scene. Filming the girls' school locale on location greatly enhances the photographic quality of this B movie and helps make it the best of the Falcon series.

28. Even Francis the talking mule got into the collegiate act when Donald O'Connor, his guardian, wins an appointment to West Point, and Francis becomes an Army mule in *Francis Goes to West Point* (Universal-International, 1952). Francis not only coaches his master to near the top of his class, he becomes the mascot of the Army football team and helps win the big

game against Navy. Once again an animal comes through as big-man-on-campus.

29. In *Dreamboat* (20th Century-Fox, 1952), Clifton Webb went on to play a college professor whose impeccable classroom image is threatened by the television release of his old movies, which featured him as a women's matinee idol. Ginger Rogers is his former leading lady, who has prompted the TV comeback which brings down the wrath of the college administration on Webb. His biggest problem, though, is his co-ed daughter, who prefers Professor Webb's academic image to that of his former movie career.

30. In 1944, *The Woman in the Window* (RKO) presaged this development when Edward G. Robinson plays a psychiatry professor who gets mixed up in a murder through his acquaintance with mystery woman Joan Bennett. Try as he might to avoid prosecution, Robinson is foiled at every turn; and the movie, under the direction of the incomparable Fritz Lang, becomes a study of what happens to a reputable member of society when respectable values deteriorate. However, the movie ends with Robinson awakening from a dream to discover to his (and the audience's) relief that he still retains his good standing.

31. Producers Releasing Corporation, one of the poverty-row studios, in fact, came forth with a gem of this type of movie in *Secrets of a Co-ed* (1942), which dramatized the then shocking affair of a college girl (Tina Thayer) and a gangster (Ric Vallin). When he is murdered, she is accused of the crime, but in a surprise ending her attorney father (played by Otto Kruger) defends her in what is probably this underrated actor's most powerful performance.

32. From the *Variety* review of *Nine Girls* (7 March 1944).

33. However, *Take Care of My Little Girl* was considerably better than a 1957 offering on the same subject called *Sorority Girl*. This was another of American-International's inane efforts directed by Roger Corman for a teenage audience.

34. In 1981, the conventions of both the horror film and the murder mystery came together in a Jamie Lee Curtis thriller called *Terror Train* (20th Century-Fox). Three years after a fraternity prank which hospitalized a student, the perpetrators find themselves being stalked by the vengeful student aboard a chartered train filled with reveling collegians attired in costume and mask.

4 Reactions, Rebellions, and Reminiscences: The 1960s–1970s

1. From the *Variety* review of *Psychomania* (19 February 1964). The theme of murder on the campus would evolve into its most sensationally graphic expression in *Stranger in the House* (Warner Brothers, 1976) in which the sisters of a sorority house are subjected to the sexually inspired fantasies of a psychopathic killer. Because the brutal Florida State University sorority house murders occurred around this time, some observers thought that life might be imitating the movies.

2. Directed by playwright Harold Pinter, *Butley*, with Alan Bates in the title role, is centered around a day in the life of Professor Butley, a teacher of English literature at a London university. The day's activities are presented in such a way, though, that the viewer is made aware of Butley's inmost self. Accordingly, his homosexuality transcends the facts of his present existence (he is currently breaking up with his former lover) to become a metaphor for his nonbeing. With Butley, then, the educational experience represents an escape from the emotional commitments of life.

3. In a similar vein, *Get Yourself a College Girl* (MGM, 1964) depended on a setting inspired by the 1960s' fascination with night spots like Whiskey a GoGo in Los Angeles. With its sketchy story based on the exposé of a proper girls' college student (Mary Ann Mobley) as the composer of several hit tunes, this movie blatantly exploited the popularity of musical combos like the Dave Clark Five and the Animals as well as individual pop singers such as Nancy Sinatra. With this kind of production, the MGM musical sank to the lowest point of its illustrious career.

4. William Peter Blatty, who would later gain a reputation as a writer of both fiction and screen horror with *The Exorcist*, wrote the screen play for *John Goldfarb*. The inspiration for the plot, he has indicated, was both the U-2 incidents over the Soviet Union and a television

showing of an old college-life movie. The fact that Notre Dame is the school author Blatty concentrates on as the one that the Arab team should play further substantiates the popular understanding of the Indiana school as the epitome of college football. However, Notre Dame officials did not take the satirical implications of this movie lightly, and brought suit against its producers. The charges have since been dropped.

5. The production of *Tall Story* as a movie provides us with an interesting study in the transformation of literary intent. Originally, in his novel, *The Homecoming Game,* Howard Nemerov dealt sensitively with the conflict between academic ethics and the commercialization of college football. Howard Lindsay and Russell Crouse retained most of this premise as the basis for the dramatic conflict of their play version, while the movie appeared to neglect any serious intent for the more popular appeal of romantic comedy of 1930s vintage.

6. Other films in this extremely popular series were *Son of Flubber* (1963), *The Computer Wore Tennis Shoes* (1970), and *The Strongest Man in the World* (1975).

7. A television series of *The Paper Chase* with John Houseman in the lead role was produced in the late 1970s. Highly praised by media critics, the series was surprisingly discontinued, but Public Broadcasting gave its sponsorship, making *The Paper Chase* the first originally commercial television series to go this route.

8. From *The Hollywood Reporter* review of *The End of the Road* (10 April 1970).

9. Nevertheless, in 1965 the movie version of Betty Smith's sentimental novel of life in a college town appeared. Obviously based on her own experiences in the university town of Chapel Hill, North Carolina during the 1930s, *Joy in the Morning* (MGM) through its evocation of life in a less complicated time looks ahead to the nostalgic mood of the collegiate film of the 1970s. Actually, the problems and concerns of a married student (Richard Chamberlain) and his wife (Yvette Mimieux) in their struggle to get him through law school come across in the manner of one of those innocuous MGM melodramas of the 1930s.

10. The movie script for *Drive, He Said* was based on Jeremy Larner's novel of the same title, which was equally controversial in its manner of expression as the film version.

11. With the title *Oh, Brotherhood,* the script for *Fraternity Row* was originally written by Charles Gary Allison as a dissertation for the cinema department at the University of Southern California.

12. Another romantic drama that drew on past collegiate experience for both this reason and for added popular appeal was the highly sentimental *If Ever I See You Again* (Columbia, 1978). Through intermittent flashbacks, we discover that Joe Brooks, a widower with two children, has never really forgotten his abortive romance with a college girl (Shelley Hack). Now, in later years, composer-musician Brooks learns from a former college acquaintance that Miss Hack is still single and living in California. On a business trip he looks her up and begins to spend some time with her, after which they both discover that they have more in common than they had ever realized back in their immature college days. Joe soon proposes marriage, but Shelley holds off, contending from her intensely independent viewpoint that she does not want so deep an involvement. However, she eventually relents and returns to Joe—the movie's emotional high point—while he is celebrating Christmas at home with his children. In spite of this film's mawkish display of sentimental feeling, it stands as no less a testimony than does *The Way We Were* to the powerful influence of personal relationships begun in college, and how the consequences of such encounters can haunt and pursue us throughout our lives.

13. The popularity of *Animal House* inspired a short-lived television spinoff called "Delta House," which featured some of the lead players in the film.

14. From *The Hollywood Reporter* review of *Fast Break* (16 February 1979).

15. From the *Variety* review of *Fast Break* (16 February 1979).

16. Melvin Frank, "Dialogue on Film," an interview in *American Film* (November 1979), 41–48.

Bibliography

The following sources—fiction and non-fiction (including contemporary film reviews, and theater productions)—are among those works which I consider to have had the greatest influence on either my thinking for the development of this book or on Hollywood's conception of the collegiate movie.

Fiction

Barbour, Ralph Henry. *The Half-back*. New York: D. Appleton & Co., 1899. This is the first novel that Barbour wrote and is representative of the kind of popular school-college fiction turned out for youthful audiences during the earlier part of this century.

Barth, John. *The End of the Road*. rev. ed. New York: Grosset & Dunlap, 1969.

Erskine, John. *Bachelor—of Arts*. Indianapolis: Bobbs-Merrill Co., 1933.

Fitch, George. *At Good Old Siwash*. Boston: Little, Brown & Co., 1911.

Fitzgerald, F. Scott. *This Side of Paradise*. New York: Charles Scribner's Sons, 1920.

Flandrau, Charles Macomb. *The Diary of a Freshman*. New York: Double-day, Page & Co., 1901.

Hall, Oakley. *The Corpus of Joe Bailey*. New York: Viking Press, 1953.

Hilton, James. *Goodbye, Mr. Chips*. Boston: Little, Brown & Co., 1934.

Johnson, Owen. *Stover at Yale*. New York: Frederick A. Stokes Co., 1912.

Kunen, James Simon. *The Strawberry Statement: Notes of a College Revolutionary*. New York: Random House, 1969.

Larner, Jeremey. *Drive, He Said*. rev. ed. New York: Bantam Books, 1971.

Lurie, Alison. *War Between the Tates*. New York: Random House, 1974.

McCarthy, Mary. *The Groves of Academe*. New York: Harcourt, Brace & Co., 1952.

Malamud, Bernard. *A New Life*. New York: Farrar, Straus & Cudahy, 1961.

Marks, Percy. *The Plastic Age*. New York: Century Co., 1924.

Nemerov, Howard. *The Homecoming Game*. New York: Simon & Schuster, 1957.

Osborn, Jr., John Jay. *The Paper Chase*. New York: Popular Library, 1979.

Rimmer, Robert H. *The Harrad Experiment*. New York: Bantam Books, 1973.

Salinger, J. D. *Franny and Zooey*. Boston: Little, Brown & Co., 1961.

Segal, Erich. *Love Story*. New York: Harper & Row, 1970.

Skinner, Cornelia Otis, and Kimbrough, Emily. *Our Hearts Were Young and Gay*. New York: Dodd, Mead & Co., 1942.

Standish, Burt L. [Gilbert Patten]. Any of the school/college stories of the popular *Frank Merriwell Series,* published by Street and Smith in *Tip Top Weekly* beginning in 1896. Various reprints are available.

Wallace, Francis. *The Big Game*. Boston: Little, Brown & Co., 1936.

———. *Huddle*. New York: Farrar, Rinehart Co., 1930.

———. *Stadium*. New York: Farrar, Rinehart Co., 1931.

———. *That's My Boy*. New York: Farrar, Rinehart Co., 1932.

Washburn, William Tucker. *Fair Harvard: A Story of American College Life*. New York: G. P. Putnam's Sons, 1869.

Willingham, Calder. *End as a Man*. New York: Vanguard Press, 1947.

Wister, Owen. *Philosophy Four: A Story of Harvard University*. New York: Macmillan Co., 1903.

Wolfe, Thomas. *Of Time and the River*. New York: Charles Scribner's Sons, 1935.

Nonfiction

Brondfield, Jerry. *Rockne: The Coach, the Man, the Legend*. New York: Random House, 1976.

Cady, Edwin H. *The Big Game: College Sports and American Life*. Knoxville: University of Tennessee Press, 1978.

Fiedler, Leslie A., and Vinocur, Jacob, eds. *The Continuing Debate: Essays on Education*. New York: St. Martin's Press, 1964.

Frank, Melvin. "Dialogue on Film." *American Film,* November 1979, pp. 41–48.

The Hollywood Reporter. Relevant reviews of collegiate films since the 1940s, as cited.

Lyons, John. *The College Novel in America*. Carbondale: Southern Illinois University Press, 1962.

Miller, Don. *"B" Movies*. New York: Curtis Books, 1973.

Parrish, James Robert. *The Great Movie Series*. Cranbury, N.J.: A. S. Barnes & Co., 1971.

Sklar, Robert. *Movie-Made America: A Social History of American Movies*. New York: Random House, 1975.

Stade, Yankee. "Football—A $50,000,000 Business." *Liberty,* October 1938, pp. 11–12.

Thurber, James. "University Days" in *My Life and Hard Times*. New York: Harper & Bros., 1933.

Variety. Relevant reviews of collegiate films since the 1920s, as cited.

Plays/Musicals

Ade, George. *The College Widow*. First New York performance was 20 September 1904 at the Garden Theatre.

————. *The Fair Co-ed*. First New York performance was 1 February 1909 at the Knickerbocker Theatre.

Albee, Edward. *Who's Afraid of Virginia Woolf?* First New York performance was 13 October 1962 at the Billy Rose Theatre.

Barry, Phillip. *Spring Dance*. First New York performance was 25 August 1936 at the Empire Theatre.

Belton, Guy, and MacGowan, Jack (book); Gershwin, George, and Gershwin, Ira (score). *Girl Crazy*. First New York performance was 14 October 1930 at the Alvin Theatre. The stage version had a dude-ranch setting rather than college.

DeMille, William, and Turnbull, Margaret. *Classmates*. First New York performance was 29 August 1907 at the Hudson Theatre.

Ephron, Phoebe and Henry. *Take Her, She's Mine*. First New York performance was 21 December 1961 at the Biltmore Theatre.

Gray, Simon. *Butley*. First New York performance was 31 October 1972 at the Morosco Theatre.

Hellman, Lillian. *The Children's Hour*. First New York performance was 20 November 1934 at Maxine Elliott's Theatre.

Kanin, Fay. *Goodbye, My Fancy*. First New York performance was 17 November 1948 at the Morosco Theatre.

Lindsay, Howard. *She Loves Me Not*. First New York performance was 20 November 1933 at the 46th Street Theatre.

———— and Crouse, Russell. *Tall Story*. First New York performance was 29 January 1959 at the Belasco Theatre.

Marion, Jr., George (book); Rogers, Richard, and Hart, Lorenz (score). *Too Many Girls*. First New York performance was 18 October 1939 at the Imperial Theatre.

Miller, Alice Duer. *The Charm School*. First New York performance was 2 August 1920 at the Bijou Theatre.

Monks, Jr., John, and Finklehoffe, Fred F. *Brother Rat*. First New York performance was 16 December 1936 at the Biltmore Theatre.

Nugent, J. C. and Elliott. *The Poor Nut*. First New York performance was 27 April 1925 at Henry Miller's Theatre.

Petitt, Wilfred H. *Nine Girls*. First New York performance was 13 January 1943 at the Longacre Theatre.

Schwab, Lawrence; Mandel, Frank, et al. *Goods News*. First New York performance was 6 September 1927 at Chanin's 46th Street Theatre.

Thurber, James, and Nugent, Elliott. *The Male Animal*. First New York performance was 9 January 1940 at the Cort Theatre.

Young, Rida Johnson. *Brown of Harvard*. First New York performance was 26 February 1906 at the Princess Theatre.

Filmography

Following is a chronological listing (1914–81) of the Hollywood films with college-oriented themes that have influenced the development of this book.

1914

Classmates (Biograph)
Strongheart (Biograph)

1915

The College Widow (Lubin)

1917

Brown of Harvard (Essanay)
The Pinch Hitter (Triangle)

1919

The Winning Stroke (Fox)

1921

Ashamed of Parents (Warner Bros.)
The Burden of Race (Reol)
Live Wires (Fox)

1923

Only 38 (Famous Players)

1924

Classmates (Inspiration)—remake of the 1914 original version

1925

The Freshman (Pathé)
The Midshipman (MGM)
The Plastic Age (Commonwealth)

1926

Brown of Harvard (MGM)—remake of the 1917 original version

The Campus Flirt (Famous Players)
The College Boob (Film Booking Office)
College Days (Tiffany)
Eyes Right! (Goodwill)
The Flaming Frontier (Universal)
One Minute to Play (Film Booking Office)
The Quarterback (Famous Players)
Readin', 'Ritin', 'Rithmetic (Artlee)

1927

College (United Artists)
The College Hero (Columbia)
The College Widow (Warner Bros.)
Dress Parade (Pathé)
The Drop Kick (First National)
The Fair Co-ed (MGM)
Naughty but Nice (First National)
The Poor Nut (First National)
Swim, Girl, Swim (Paramount)
West Point (MGM)

1928

Annapolis (Pathé)
The Cheer Leader (Lumas)
Hold 'em Yale! (Pathé)
The Olympic Hero (Supreme)
Red Lips (Universal)
Varsity (Paramount)

1929

College Coquette (First National)
College Love (Universal)—this was a feature film compilation of *The Collegians* shorts
The Duke Steps Out (MGM)
The Forward Pass (First National)
Hot Stuff (First National)
Redskin (Paramount)
Salute (Fox)
The Sophomore (Pathé)
So This Is College (MGM)
Sweetie (Paramount)
The Wild Party (Paramount)
Words and Music (Fox)

1930

College Lovers (First National)
Good News (MGM)
Maybe It's Love (Warner Bros.)

1931

Confessions of a Co-ed (Paramount)
Girls Demand Excitement (Fox)
Local Boy Makes Good (First National)
Maker of Men (Columbia)

The Spirit of Notre Dame (Universal)
Touchdown (Paramount)

1932

Age of Consent (RKO)
The All-American (Universal)
Horse Feathers (Paramount)
Huddle (MGM)
That's My Boy (Columbia)

1933

College Coach (Warner Bros.)
College Humor (Paramount)
Midshipman Jack (RKO)
Saturday's Millions (Universal)
The Sweetheart of Sigma Chi (Monogram)

1934

The Band Plays On (MGM)
College Rhythm (Paramount)
Finishing School (RKO)
Flirtation Walk (Warner Bros.)
Gridiron Flash (RKO)
She Loves Me Not Paramount)
Student Tour (MGM)

1935

Annapolis Farewell (Paramount)
Bachelor of Arts (Fox)
College Scandal (Paramount)
Hold 'em Yale (Paramount)
Old Man Rhythm (RKO)
Shipmates Forever (Warner Bros.)

1936

The Big Game (RKO)
College Holiday (Paramount)
Collegiate (Paramount)
Freshman Love (Warner Bros.)
Pigskin Parade (20th Century-Fox)
Rose Bowl (Paramount)
We Went to College (MGM)

1937

Hold 'em Navy (Paramount)
Life Begins in College (20th Century-Fox)
Murder Goes to College (Paramount)
Navy Blue and Gold (MGM)
Over the Goal (Warner Bros.)
Rosalie (MGM)
Varsity Show (Warner Bros.)

1938

Brother Rat (Warner Bros.)

Campus Confessions (Paramount)
Campus Mystery (Columbia)
College Swing (Paramount)
Duke of West Point (United Artists)
Freshman Year (Universal)
The Gladiator (Columbia)
Hold That Co-ed (20th Century-Fox)
My Lucky Star (20th Century-Fox)
Spring Madness (MGM)
Start Cheering (Columbia)
Swing It, Professor (Ambassador)
Swing That Cheer (Universal)
Touchdown, Army (Paramount)
Vivacious Lady (RKO)

1939

Dancing Co-ed (MGM)
Million Dollar Legs (Paramount)
Naughty but Nice (Warner Bros.)
$1,000 a Touchdown (Paramount)
Sorority House (RKO)
These Glamour Girls (MGM)
Winter Carnival (United Artists)

1940

Forty Little Mothers (MGM)
Knute Rockne—All-American (Warner Bros.)
The Quarterback (Paramount)
Those Were the Days (Paramount)—former title, *At Good Old Siwash*
Too Many Girls (RKO)
Yesterday's Heroes (20th Century-Fox)

1941

All-American Co-ed (United Artists)
Harmon of Michigan (Columbia)
Let's Go Collegiate (Monogram)
Naval Academy (Universal)
Rise and Shine (20th Century-Fox)
Sis Hopkins (Republic)
Sweetheart of the Campus (Columbia)
Zis Boom Bah (Monogram)

1942

Andy Hardy's Double Life (MGM)
Blondie Goes to College (Columbia)
Harvard, Here I Come (Columbia)
The Male Animal (Warner Bros.)
Secrets of a Co-ed (Producers Releasing Corporation)
Smith of Minnesota (Columbia)
The Spirit of Stanford (Columbia)
Sweater Girl (Paramount)
Ten Gentlemen from West Point (20th Century-Fox)

1943

Campus Rhythm (Monogram)
The Falcon and the Co-eds (RKO)
Girl Crazy (MGM)
The Iron Major (RKO)
Young Ideas (MGM)

1944

Andy Hardy's Blonde Trouble (MGM)
Bathing Beauty (MGM)
Nine Girls (Columbia)
The Woman in the Window (RKO)

1945

Here Come the Co-eds (Universal)

1946

Do You Love Me (20th Century-Fox)
Love Laughs at Andy Hardy (MGM)
Our Hearts Were Young and Gay (Paramount)

1947

Betty Co-ed (Columbia)
Good News (MGM)
The Spirit of West Point (Film Classics)
The Trouble with Women (Paramount)

1948

Apartment for Peggy (20th Century-Fox)
Family Honeymoon (Universal-International)

1949

The Accused (Paramount)
Father Was a Fullback (20th Century-Fox)
It Happens Every Spring (20th Century-Fox)
Mr. Belvedere Goes to College (20th Century-Fox)
Mother Is a Freshman (20th Century-Fox)
Yes Sir, That's My Baby (Universal-International)

1950

The Jackie Robinson Story (Eagle-Lion)
Peggy (Universal-International)
The West Point Story (Warner Bros.)
A Woman of Distinction (Columbia)

1951

Bedtime for Bonzo (Universal-International)
Goodbye, My Fancy (Warner Bros.)
Jim Thorpe—All-American (Warner Bros.)
Saturday's Hero (Columbia)
Take Care of My Little Girl (20th Century-Fox)
That's My Boy (Paramount)

1952

About Face (Warner Bros.)
Bonzo Goes to College (Universal-International)
Dreamboat (20th Century-Fox)
Francis Goes to West Point (Universal-International)
Hold That Line (Monogram)
The Rose Bowl Story (Monogram)
She's Working Her Way Through College (Warner Bros.)

1953

The Affairs of Dobie Gillis (MGM)
The All-American (Universal-International)
Crazylegs (Republic)
Trouble Along the Way (Warner Bros.)

1955

How to Be Very, Very Popular (20th Century-Fox)
The Long Gray Line (Columbia)

1957

The Strange One (Columbia)

1958

Mardi Gras (20th Century-Fox)
Monster on the Campus (Universal-International)
Teacher's Pet (Paramount)

1960

College Confidential (Universal-International)
High Time (20th Century-Fox)
Sex Kittens Go to College (Allied Artists)
Tall Story (Warner Bros.)

1961

The Absent-Minded Professor (Buena Vista)
Tammy Tell Me True (Universal-International)

1963

The Nutty Professor (Paramount)
Son of Flubber (Buena Vista)
Take Her, She's Mine (20th Century-Fox)

1964

For Those Who Think Young (United Artists)
Get Yourself a College Girl (MGM)
Psychomania (Victoria)
The Young Lovers (MGM)

1965

John Goldfarb, Please Come Home (20th Century-Fox)
Joy in the Morning (MGM)

1966

Who's Afraid of Virginia Woolf? (Warner Bros.)

1967

    C'mon Let's Live a Little (Paramount)

1969

    The Sterile Cuckoo (Paramount)

1970

    Adam at Six A.M. (National General)
    The Computer Wore Tennis Shoes (Buena Vista)
    The End of the Road (Allied Artists)
    Getting Straight (Columbia)
    Love Story (Paramount)
    R.P.M. (Columbia)
    The Strawberry Statement (MGM)

1971

    Carnal Knowledge (Embassy)
    Drive, He Said (Columbia)

1973

    Class of '44 (Warner Bros.)
    The Harrad Experiment (Cinema Arts)
    The Paper Chase (20th Century-Fox)
    The Way We Were (Columbia)

1974

    The Gambler (Paramount)

1975

    The Strongest Man in the World (Buena Vista)

1976

    Stranger in the House (Warner Bros.)

1977

    First Love (Paramount)
    Fraternity Row (Paramount)
    One on One (Warner Bros.)

1978

    Animal House (Universal City)
    If Ever I See You Again (Columbia)

1979

    Fast Break (Columbia)
    Lost and Found (Columbia)

1980

    Foolin' Around (Columbia)

1981

    Dirty Tricks (Avco Embassy)
    Terror Train (20th Century-Fox)

Index

Illustrations are indicated by boldface type.